Peach Pits at my Door

And other adventures

Peach Pits at my Door

And other adventures

John Jopes

Dragonflyer
PRESS

This work originally appeared in the Inland Valley Daily Bulletin.
Reprinted with permission of the publishers.
Copyright © 1996 by the Inland Valley Daily Bulletin.

All rights reserved. No part of this book may be used or reproduced in any manner whatsoever without written permission except for brief quotations embodied in attributed reviews and articles.

Published by
Dragonflyer Press
521 North Mountain Avenue, Suite A
Upland, California 91786

	LIBRARY OF CONGRESS CATALOGING-IN-PUBLICATION DATA
979.4	Jopes, John Leland, 1929 Jun. 28-
JOP	Peach Pits at my door and other adventures / John Jopes ; introduction by Barry Morrow. - 1st ed. Upland, Ca. : Dragonflyer Press ©1996.
	726 p. ; 127 cm.
	"This work originally appeared in the *Inland Valley Daily Bulletin*."
	Summary: A collection of selected newspaper columns about the history, people, places and events of the Inland Valley area of southern California.
	ISBN 0-944933-06-8
	1. American newspapers - California - Inland Valley - Sections, columns, etc. - Facsimiles 2. Inland Valley (Calif.)- History - Sources I. Title
	979.4-dc20

Book design by
Carolyn Hayes Uber and Norma Favila

Jacket design by
Sue Campbell

Author photo by Shelby Forrest

First Edition: October 1996

10 9 8 7 6 5 4 3 2 1

Printed in Hong Kong

*For
Anna and Harrison
and
Curt*

Author's Note

The content of this book is a collection of selected newspaper columns I wrote between January, 1992, and July, 1994. Although many of them are commentary in nature, they could be better described as small stories having to do with people, places, events and the history of the Inland Valley.

Most are based on experiences I have had, and what I have learned, as a newspaperman in the valley since 1955. A few of the columns, however, describe events in earlier parts of my life.

The accounts of historical events and people of the valley could not have been written without the help of books by local authors Esther Boulton Black, Bob Schmidt and Martha Gaines Stoebe. Particularly helpful to me was the work of Donald L. Clucas, *Light Over the Mountain—A History of the Rancho Cucamonga Area* (Revised Edition).

In the main text of this book I have made no attempt to update the columns from their original version. But I have added an epilogue that offers later information on a few of them.

All of the columns were originally published in the *Inland Valley Daily Bulletin*.

— John Jopes
Upland, California
September, 1996

Introduction

It was noon, we were sitting in a comfy outdoor restaurant, waiting for our hot turkey sandwiches to arrive. He was showing me the discoloration on his forearm, a large splotchy contusion, the result, he said, of mis-hitting a golf ball the day before. Being an inveterate hacker myself, I pressed him for details: could he remember the mechanics of that particular shot, the precise moment of his backswing or follow-through when whatever it was that went wrong . . . went wrong?

No, but he could recall with buoyant clarity the blueness of the sky that morning, and an earlier, almost magically-struck six-iron that sent his ball fluttering to the putting green like a pigeon to a park.

Clearly, John Jopes the golfer would have to concentrate harder.

We ruminated a while on the mysteries of the human body, and the greater mysteries of the ancient game of golf. Modern medicine had banished smallpox from the planet, but the scourge of the weekend slice remains pandemic.

This was just my second encounter with John—my second hot turkey sandwich—yet already I felt a deep kinship with the man. To begin with, we were both writers, though of vastly different stripes: he from journalism; I from Hollywood. A good journalist, we agreed, must tell the truth, while a good screenwriter must only seem to. He thought my job was harder.

We were meeting to discuss the details of a publishing project—this one—and as writers do, we digressed. Soon we were back to golf, considering its endless provocations and the curious way it reveals the true (and not always flattering) character of a player. John said that while he could still play the game, he'd lost some distance off the tee and now prefers the more forgiving company of retired golf partners. It is a brisk walk and a fair day in the sun he seeks, not combat. He confessed to not even mind seeing his ball plop into the middle of a lake now and then, there being a certain elegance to such an event.

My guess is that even in his more competitive days, John was never unduly concerned about sailing off into the rough or going out-of-bounds, for it was there, deep in the tangled thicket and out of view, that he was apt to make some important discovery, like a snake hole or a hawk's nest or a four-iron bent in two. And this in turn might lead to the one thing he was endlessly in search of—not a golf ball, but a story.

And so it has always been for John Jopes, journalist and storyteller. His aim was to take you, his guest/reader, off the main highway and down a narrow road and through a small doorway and onto an old sofa and into the heart of a complete stranger who just might teach you something. And when you'd come to the end of a piece with a Jopes byline, you felt you'd rediscovered a truth you'd always known. He made it that easy to learn.

A good writer is never at rest. Every passing person, place, and thing holds the promise, sometimes the obligation, of a story. Like the death of a steel plant, or a car that only makes left turns; like the irresistible charm of a blonde named Ginger, or the poignant demise of a town's last resident. Triumphs and tragedies. Laughter and tears. With a few left turns.

Golf has a handicap system designed to equalize players. The rest of the time, we rely on poets and artists to provide that perspective, to reveal the little things in a big story, and the big things in a little story. No one ever did this better than Jopes. With economy of style and wit and warmth, with respect for all whom he encountered, he wrote so that we might see ourselves in our neighbor's struggle, making us more alike than not.

Our lunch was over, our plates picked clean. As we were leaving, he casually mentioned another interest of his, gardening, a subject about which I knew next to nothing. He said the older he gets the more he enjoys it, like a brisk walk on a fair day. As I drove home I imagined him out in his garden, down on his knees planting and weeding, digging and digging, turning the earth over and over, for that is his way.

—Barry Morrow

Contents

Looking For A Valley 1
A Countryside In Flight 3
The Car 5
Requiem For Days Of Thunder 7
Donnie 9
Peach Pits At My Door 11
Getting Along 13
These Guys Won't Forget 15
Dorothy Grant 17
Helpless 19
The Barber Shop 21
The Quakes 23
The Shoes 25
Shopping Quietly 27
Old Dogs And Children 29
A Favor For Mah Wong 31
Dorothy Wisely 33
Dako 35
Big Ol' Virgil 39
Running Through The Night 41
Generation Of Vipers? 43
Mary And OPARC 45
Julie And Other Angels 47
Mickey 49
An Interchange for Mr. Mikesell 51
Woody 53
A.T. 55
Santa Claus. 57
Claremont's Quiet Place 59
Don Drysdale 61
The Beach 63

Centro Basco	65
Tell A Child	69
Pigeon's Roost, AKA Pomona	71
Death In The Texas Sand	73
Ima's Trophy	75
An Angel In The Night	77
Fred	79
The Village On The Hill	81
She's Still A Lady	83
Phillips Mansion	85
Winter On The Mountain	87
Nice Pills	89
Lindbergh In Our Valley	91
A Day In The Sun	93
Remember The Guns	95
A Stillness On The Land	97
Lois	99
The Doctor	101
Birding	103
Tapia's Treasure	105
Hondo In San Dimas	107
Diana's World	109
A Day At The Pump	111
The Battle Of Chino	115
A Visit On A Corner	117
John Jamerson	121
Ramon And The Language	123
Dogs and Me	125
Uncle Billy Rubottom	127
Puerto Penasco	129
Lucille	131
This Town's Name Just Won't Die	133
Seely	135
The Floods	137

Ginger	139
The Chaffey House	141
A Word That's Gone With The Wind	143
Diamond Bar	145
What's In Upland's Name?	147
Kelly's Mine And Mountain	149
24 Tortillas	151
Boris	153
The Monroe Street Parade	155
Leaving The Rest To Others	157
Epilogue	159

Looking For A Valley

I had been away.

I'd been out of circulation for so many years that contacts with my friends had become stretched thin, and my long-kept pallbearer list had diminished to about three shy of a full complement.

That, I began to fear, could lead to the peculiar prospect of my making that last somber trip down the aisle on a tilt.

So I decided to return.

Our home actually remained, but my absences were so frequent that it is was almost as if I lived elsewhere.

When I left this valley, much of it was referred to as the "West End." That term supposedly was justified by the fact that this part of the world is, more or less, on the west end of San Bernardino County.

In my search for the valley I learned that it is people more than it is space.

There were other names. "Pomona Valley" and "Chino Valley" were widely and proudly applied to describe the expanse serving as the first carpet of land east of the Los Angeles Basin.

Now that I am back, it seems those names have largely yielded to new nomenclature—the Inland Valley.

Fair enough.

The other day I set out to find it.

The valley's physical dimension is not complicated. Looking east from the manicured campus of Cal Poly on Kellogg Hill, the Inland Valley can be viewed unobstructed. All of it.

From there, the freeway curls off the hill, then slices through the freeway interchange as if hurrying away from Los Angeles in search of some better place.

Changes have settled in during my absence. When I left, for instance, Fontana was a beer and hamburger town. A maker of steel. A place more of paper shades than curtains.

As in Sandburg's *Chicago*, Fontana had big shoulders. The town is different now, yet it has a proud past and a rose-colored future.

To the north, citrus groves still protruded down the alluvial fan as far south as Foothill Boulevard, and beyond, in parts of Upland.

Those grand, green ranks barely hung on then. They persevered though, exemplifying a courageous defiance of what was to come.

But the trees seemed to be in some sort of sorrowful retreat. They're gone now. And the valley's cultural differences are more evident. In some places it's "Please excuse me." In others it's *"Perdoneme"*.

Is that strange? Not at all. What's precious about where we all live is the pure diversity of the place. Although our individual communities are bound by geography, they are free in the pursuit of their own identities.

In my search for the valley I learned that it is people more than it is space.

It is Bill Graber, who was born in Ontario 81 years ago this month and has seen many of his dreams fulfilled.

It is Gabriel Lopez-Plasencia, who was born at Doctors Hospital in Montclair Wednesday, and has yet to dream at all.

It is Imelda and Martin, Gabriel's parents, whose future is the child in their arms.

It is Pomona Police Sgt. Ronald McDonald, whose quiet dedication earns a respect on the street as well as in the squad room of his own station.

It is Roma Carpenter, a nurse at Chino Hospital, who, I am told, often cares more for her patients than for herself.

And it is the five brave people, who recently became the city of Chino Hills first council members. The are Gwenn Norton-Perry, Mike Wickman, Gary Larson, Jim Thalman and Ed Graham, who have set aside the ecstasy of recent elections so they can tackle the challenging arithmetic of making a brand new city work.

I pondered these things as I concluded my hunt and returned home.

Later I encountered my neighbor, Schumway. He was ministering to a wounded sprinkler head in his front yard.

"Where you been this time?" he asked. "Texas?"

"No, I don't do that much anymore. I've been out looking for a valley."

"Did you find one?"

"I sure did. It's a good place. And I picked up a couple of ideas for pallbearers, too." I said.

"You're too much," ol' Schumway replied. "I've missed those kind of dumb remarks. I'm glad you're back."

"Me, too" I said.

A Countryside In Flight

The countryside is not where it used to be.

Gone.

In its place are people and their houses.

A Sunday afternoon ride to see the country has become more of an undertaking than an outing. It's akin to a search. A whole landscape is in flight, and what's left of it is moving out ahead of the chase.

It's as if it were in a frightful attempt to outrun something that surely will devour it.

The other day I decided to find the caboose of it all—the tag end of "out in the country."

I was looking for real country. It would have weighty trees, spring grass, old farmhouses, and sagging barns with sun slanting through where it shouldn't.

The trees were planted in a snugged-together manner so they could serve as enormous fenders against mean wind.

All of this could be found at the edge of every downtown in the valley a few years ago, but now what is left of it is in the east and on the mountain slopes.

I felt that if I could find some old windbreaks I would be in the country. What is left of these windbreaks (sometimes called hedgerows) now stand as shrines to decades past when there was purpose to their long, straight lines.

These great rows were long ranks of stately eucalyptus trees. The trees were planted in a snugged-together manner so they could serve as enormous fenders against mean wind.

The thunderous gales (called Santanas then) were sucked through the canyons and sent beating against an ocean of citrus groves.

The tight rows of eucalyptus held every grove in protective embrace.

There were tens of thousands of them in the valley, and from lower reaches they appeared to be a forest of eucalyptus. From the hills above they looked like a patchwork of seams in a giant green quilt.

It was overcast and cool the day of my search for the country. The mountain range was gone in the clouds as I drove east along Highland Avenue through Rancho Cucamonga.

Not until I approached Etiwanda Avenue did I see a full row of windbreak. Then there were more, although there were stumps among them telling me people in search of firewood had gone about their business there.

A turn south on Etiwanda took me through a vestige of another time.

There were the ancient farm houses, a flock of sheep pulling at grass in a quiet meadow, and some old outbuildings—tired now. Yet nearby were tracts of handsome new dwellings.

The windbreaks were there in sporadic lines, but hardly a grove was left.

I stopped on Victoria Street to visit Terry Frost, whose family has been on that land for four generations.

His great-grandfather, George Frost, a one-time associate of the Chaffey Brothers, settled the land in 1882 and farmed it with citrus.

George was Etiwanda's first postmaster.

Terry's father and grandfather also served as postmasters.

The house in which Terry lives was built by his parents, and his cousin, Jim Frost, who was Rancho Cucamonga's first mayor. He lives four houses east of Terry in a home built more than 90 years ago.

Terry talked of the old days—the groves, the cold, the wind and the smudging. And he lamented the time when the sensitive environment and the cost of land brought an end to King Citrus.

From the Frost place I traveled north past Highland up the slope until the curb played out. More meadows, trees and open space up there.

Finally, past the water plant, all evidence of cultivation vanished.

I turned around when nothing was left but sage, rock, rabbits and maybe a bit of buckwheat.

Looking down on the valley I could see the country I had come to find. It lay at my feet then rolled out and feathered itself into an expanse of homes, streets, parks, schools and ample signs of industry.

It was quiet up there in the brush.

I turned to go from that silent slope and noticed a sign squeaking in the breeze. It said: "Coming soon—a planned residential community."

It will be a nice place to live.

The Car

About this time of year, the welcome sun of summer moves my memory. And images of my 19th June come and go as if they were caught in the twist of a kaleidoscope.

I was a college student then, immersed in the world's wonder. I was long on eagerness to grab life and joy with vigor. My reservoir of good sense, however, did not run very deep.

My understanding of life's great priorities was not necessarily distorted, but my full definition of them was yet to come. I was still to answer maturity's call.

Looking back, I believe that in that 19th year I may have been intellectually tanning myself on an over-the-horizon island, out of sight of life's realities.

It was nice out there.

> *The steering wheel came off in my hands. Just came off.*

No calamity had yet brought any temporary ruin to my life, and I regarded tomorrow as something to occupy others' concerns. I did not look much beyond the end of the day.

The life I lived was what most people would have described as carefree, but my father believed I was irresponsible. My mother was kinder and more understanding.

College was, by my reckoning, a good place to have fun.

I had the only car on campus that apparently had termites. The car, for which I had paid $75, was old enough to vote.

Parts of its chassis were manufactured with wood, and that's where I assumed the termites lived. I sometimes marveled at the fact they were eating themselves out of a place to live.

I was told the motor mounts on the old car had long ago served their best purpose, so the engine sort of rose and fell in a furious struggle to revolve around itself.

This unhappy mechanical malady caused a strange electrical malfunction, and the headlights flickered on and off every time I turned right. If the turn was a prolonged one, and I had the steering wheel cranked to the right for a sufficient time, a fuse would expire and the lights would go out for good.

Therefore, during nighttime driving I learned to go everywhere using left turns only. I also carried extra fuses just in case I turned right during a mental lapse.

"Why are we turning left here?" a passenger new to my car once asked.

"Never mind, we'll get there."

Actually, I became reasonably adept at getting around with left turns. I could leave my dorm, cross the campus, get to the rathskeller and back about as fast as students who had cars that would turn both ways.

Once I asked a guy in a service station if I should change the oil, and he admonished me not to do it.

"Man, that old oil is what is holding your car up. I wouldn't even wash it if I were you."

After my sophomore year, my roommate and I drove north where we were to work in the Oregon woods for the summer. We were somewhere north of Sacramento in that expansive land of rice when, for some reason, the steering wheel came off in my hands. Just came off.

"Here, take this," I said to my roommate, handing him the steering wheel. Then I grabbed hold of the small spokes that remained, and kept driving.

Later a cop stopped us at the Shasta Dam parking lot.

"Hi there, officer."

"Where's your steering wheel?"

"The steering wheel? It's in the trunk."

"OK, but be careful," he said as he walked away.

"I guess he just wanted to know where it is," my roommate said.

The old car finally died just north of Grants Pass. I mean expired, passed on.

My companion and I pushed the car into a lumberyard parking lot and just left it there. We completed our trip to Riddle, Oregon, on a Greyhound bus.

Later, when I learned it was illegal to abandon a vehicle, I called the lumberyard and asked the guy who answered the phone if he wanted to buy the car. He said he wasn't interested.

So I gave it to him.

Requiem For Days Of Thunder

"So you want to go to work in the mill, boy?", he said to the 17-year-old. *The man of sweat was whole union—he was a big, jowly, smoked a cigar and was Wallace Beery rough. "You gonna do good work? Be a good union man like your dad? You ain't gonna give us no sass? Good, then you can go to work in the coke ovens tomorrow."*

The din of the blast furnaces and their fierce eruptions were the great beat of the mill. And the mill itself was the industrial throb of an entire county.

With its 10,000 steelworkers, the grand plant churned along like a juggernaut in a sea of sage. All 1,100 acres of it stretched out in the flat of the valley west of Fontana.

This was Kaiser Steel in the high water of industrial health and vigor. It chugged, pulsated and exploded 24 hours a day, 365 days a year, its blast furnaces turning out 10,000 tons of iron every day.

The people of the mill were as hard as the metal they worked. They believed—and behaved—as if there were steelworkers in this world, and then there was everyone else.

Steelmen were somehow apart from the rest. They worked the mill—and lived as well—as a fraternity of muscled men, sweat, roar, goggles, and fire.

They worked the mill—and lived as well—as a fraternity of muscled men, sweat, roar, goggles, and fire.

A man who knew this molten world of steel and noise is the 17-year-old-old boy who took that job in the coke ovens.

That was 42 years ago.

The boy is Gerry Fawcett, who worked himself out of the ovens, through college and threaded his way to the high country of Kaiser management.

Gerry now is responsible for what is left of the plant. He is, he says with a telling bit of grief, seeing to the burial of a giant.

For the mill is a corpse now. It is a great silent hulk sprawling out as if it were lying on its back waiting for scavengers to play a part in a mournful requiem.

Only wreckage remains in the wake of dismantlers and salvage crews.

The noise of the once immense fire and might is gone. So are 10,000 people, leaving behind a silence that settles on the broken plant with its own kind of thunder.

The ghostly quiet pressed down on Gerry and me as we walked among toppled stacks and tons of reinforcement bar that is bent into twisted and crazy sculpture. Work stations stood stark in the open, their rusted benches and chairs looking as if they had been untended for a century.

Tumbleweeds by the hundreds have come to occupy the place. They are the new tenants now.

Loose brick and mortar lie in great mounds as if a mighty bomb had done its work here. The feeling of death of a vibrant time was everywhere.

A nudged brick tumbled into a roofless pit that once was the fired and neatly enclosed slab mill. The fall of the brick was the only sound that Gerry and I heard, and I thought there might have been an echo to it.

The mill was built during World War II's grimmest days. It pounded out steel plates for Henry J. Kaiser, who was laying a keel per day for Liberty Ships at his Vallejo and Portland yards.

The plant muscled into post-war years and was King of Steel in the West.

But a treacherous web was spun by nature's intolerant environment, industrial competition from the Orient, and a fatal paralysis finally exhausted the giant's fiscal strength.

Kaiser Steel died in that snare, and the mill's roar rattled down to silence in 1983, its furnaces forever banked.

Now we are told the future will erase the rest, and there will be nothing left of the mill. The rebar, bricks, fallen stacks, slag, dead ovens and all the twists and rust that tell us of another age, will be gone.

But a Phoenix will rise from the once red maelstrom, according to Gerry's view of things. There will be clean, tall office buildings, landscape, people, jobs and a new and better life.

"I look forward to that," Gerry said softly.

And this time I sensed no grief in his talk.

Donnie

I have heard from Edna Hector of Alta Loma only twice in my life.

The first time was 19 years ago. It was a compassionate letter written to express Edna's thanks to some people who had shown her family a special sort of kindness.

Edna, her husband, DeWitt, and their son, Donnie, lived in Upland at the time. Her letter prompted me to write about it. Here is part of what I wrote:

There are some who have come to know a very blessed brand of love. It is that which is given to a boy who needs help.

The rather wondrous relationship might be adequately described by the inscription at Boys Town: "He ain't heavy, Father, he's my brother."

> *"We have been taking care of that boy for 28 years, and I wouldn't take a billion dollars for him."*

And everyone, of course, is everyone's brother (or sister). DeWitt and Edna Hector know this to be true, and they know that kind of love.

They give it constantly to their 28-year-old son, Donnie. When Donnie was an infant, an illness left him with a hopelessly damaged brain.

His body, though, remained strong. He grew and physically matured, but his mind remained behind to occupy a world of it's own, never to be shared with anyone.

Physicians suggested that the Hectors institutionalize their child, but DeWitt and Edna rejected the suggestion outright. Donnie was their baby, they said—the last of seven sons—and they considered nothing more than to care for him and love him.

"We have been taking care of that boy for 28 years, and I wouldn't take a billion dollars for him," DeWitt said. Then the Hectors told me a story.

There were some particularly kind people involved in the story, but their names were not known to the Hectors. Could I find out who they are? Could I pass along to them the Hectors' gratitude?

It seems that several nights ago, one of the Hectors awakened. It was 2 a.m. It was then they discovered a frightful thing—Donnie was gone.

His condition prohibits him from expanding his world beyond the family home. He had never been out alone before. Locks had seen to that. But this time Donnie managed to unlock a door and step outside into the night while his parents slept.

Within a few seconds he was lost, confused, frightened and cold.

He wandered out of his neighborhood, and later was found in the middle of Eighth Street by Upland police officers.

As they approached to investigate, Donnie broke and ran, but the officers stopped him with no trouble.

"My God, they could have killed him," Edna told me. "He's a big boy, and when he ran away his action could have caused officers to strike him—maybe even shoot him."

"When we discovered he was missing I immediately called the Upland Police station," Edna said. "The very nice lady assured me our son was fine and at San Antonio Hospital."

The officers had taken Donnie there, and stayed with him for more than an hour—until parents and son could be reunited.

I accepted the task of learning the names of the officers so the Hectors could thank those "particularly kind people."

Actually, there were six of them: dispatchers Arlene Nelson and Sarah Clark, plus officers Tom Balogh, Robert Reever, Dennis Segur and Sgt. Virgil Bramblett.

"There are not enough words for my husband and me to express our deepest appreciation and gratitude to these wonderful officers," Edna wrote.

I felt the strong sense that the helpful people from the Police Department learned that Donnie ain't heavy. And neither are his parents.

The second time I heard from Edna was last week. She called my office to let me know that Donnie died the other day, and she thought I might want to know. I appreciate her call.

It is somehow comforting to learn that Donnie lived his whole life without being denied parental love.

And he will never be lost again.

Peach Pits At My Door

If I live long enough, and the peanut brittle holds out, kids will no longer roam the streets. Public tranquillity will prevail.

Street gangs will disappear from the earth and, as the dinosaurs did, dissolve into mystery.

There will be peace in the valley.

How do I know this? Because eager young people who call at our door tell us so. They implore us to purchase their peanut brittle.

"It's to help keep me off the streets and out of gangs. And if I sell enough I get to go to Six Flags." They all say the same thing.

I will not assert here that the line of these peddlers of sweet sin is unbroken, but the gaps in it are relatively short. By my count, I have already kept a small regiment of young people off the streets. And I assume most have gone on to theme parks somewhere.

My neighbor and ol' buddy, Schumway, came over last weekend to help me overcome the weariness of a two-week business trip. We were watching Michael Jordan play basketball while nine other guys on the court looked on.

The doorbell rang. It was a brittle salesman. I cannot deny these fresh, young people. Their pitch, somehow, seems to me to be earnest, not forced.

> *They stood there looking up at me with smiles as wide as happy jack-o'-lanterns.*

The magic of youth looking to older folk for help does its work on me, and I see a genuine need there. Right or wrong. So I buy.

I also sadly wonder if the salespersons are Oliver Twists working at the will of some Fagin hidden away counting the kids' dollars before he fetches more peanut brittle for them to sell.

"Maybe if enough people in this world would just buy this stuff," I told Schumway, "there wouldn't be any kids on the street at all."

"I know," he said, "They'd all be up at Six Flags."

Better than being into mischief, I thought.

The next day three little girls called at the front door with their own measure of magic and a different product to sell. They stood there looking up at me with smiles as wide as happy jack-o'-lanterns.

They appeared to me as if none of them had used up more than a half dozen years. Seven at the most. I looked In the background for parents hovering nearby as protective agents. I saw none.

Perhaps they were there, but out of sight. Each of the kids carried small Ziploc baggies, and in each bag were a few peach pits.

"Mister, how would you like to buy a peach seed?"

"What would I do with it?"

"Take care of it, and it will turn into a tree."

"How much?"

"Twenty-five cents."

That is considerably less than the $5 I pay for peanut brittle that I never eat, I thought.

I suspected these salesladies were not particularly interested in staying off the streets. Or even going to Six Flags. I guessed they just wanted to experience the thrill of the sale.

And, of course, the quarter that would go with it.

"Maybe I should buy three," I said.

"You only need to buy one. We sell as a group."

Ah, a partnership, I thought. That's nice.

I wanted to ask their names and where they live, but I calculated by their ages, their fathers were probably young hunks who are 6 feet 13, and when they're not pumping iron are paying calls on old guys who have asked the names and addresses of their daughters.

"These are really nice seeds," said the child who appeared to be the youngest.

"I'll take one."

One of the bags was quickly unzipped, and I was handed a scrubbed and dried peach pit.

"And don't forget—you need to water it three times a day," said the littlest one as the trio turned to leave. "It's like magic."

Later, my wife asked, as she stood by the kitchen sink, "What's this peach seed doing here?"

"If I water it three times a day it will turn into a tree."

"What are you talking about?"

"Magic," I said, "just magic."

Getting Along

> *"Korean-owned radio station donated food to a black church, and a Korean-American was named co-chair of a parade honoring the Rev. Martin Luther King in gestures intended to ease ethnic tension."*
> —News item, the *Daily Bulletin*

My father often told us that my mother's people were blue-bellied Yankees.

And, according to my father's Dixie definition, my mother was one, too. But I never heard him call *her* that.

His grandfather was a Confederate officer. My mother's ancestors opposed the South's uprising, so I was raised in a home in which that military conflict was alternately referred to as "The War Between the States," and "The Civil War."

I thought that they were two separate wars until I was a pretty big kid.

It made school tough for a while. But despite those sharply polarized (even ethnic) backgrounds, a commendatory harmony prevailed in our family.

The war was over.

Harmony is not always found in our kaleidoscopic world— or even in our own valley.

Discord sometimes muscles compassion and understanding aside. Murders it in fact—literally.

I submit there are more people who respect and like one another than who do not.

But legions of people are not encumbered by barriers and ugliness. They just get along. And that doesn't make much news.

The above quoted newspaper item is a notable exception.

With no intent to diminish the real problems of human relationships, I submit there are more people who respect and like one another than who do not.

There is a real saucepan of people in our valley. Most of them mix very well.

Every Saturday morning, for example, I, with my Germanic background, and my 10-year-old dog of Russian ancestry, drive over to Pixie's for doughnuts.

Serving me (and 67 soccer players' mothers) each week is Moun Chau.

She has a smile as soft as filtered sun on a morning meadow.

Maun is beautiful, and though she may not suspect it, my Saturday mornings are made better by a visit with her than by the warm goodness she wraps up for us to take home.

Maun is rooted to the Far East, a half a globe away from my own start.

And there's Ramon Flores—he helps me with our yard work. Ramon is an accomplished tender of things that grow.

He is from Old Mexico. His mother still lives there, and Ramon keeps in contact with her with a ham radio.

When we need buon gusto or pepperoncini I travel to Claro's. The place is so Italian it somehow seems wrong to go in there without buying something right from Milan.

Lucia Spina is my keeper at Claro's, and she waits on me with care.

She and her fellow workers seem to be suspended in a perpetual state of fun and conversation—with patrons as well as with themselves.

I count Maun, Ramon and Lucia among those whose company is a pleasure.

And there are others like them—such as Amir Pourteymoor, Joe Y. Hung, John McBride, Mary Roberts and Chung Yoo, all of whom regularly brush my life in some way.

These people's beginnings are as scattered as leaves in an autumn breeze—just as everyone's are.

A branch of my own family has been in this country since the 1700s when they came ashore from fishing boats on the coast of Virginia.

They wandered west through Tennessee, Missouri, and finally arrived in California in this century.

My wife is but a single generation removed from Lincoln County, England.
Her family settled mostly in the Plains states of America.

And I am glad they did—I think it would trouble me to tell our children their mother's people were blue-bellied Yankees.

There's harmony in our home, and I like to keep it that way.

These Guys Won't Forget

Almost by accident I made an a oblique reference to the Korean War the other day in the presence of a 20-year-old.

I might as well have mentioned the Boxer Rebellion. Or "54-40 or Fight." Or the sinking of the *Panay*.

My young companion was more familiar with General Pickett's adventure at Gettysburg than he was with the Korean War in its entirety.

I think he believes Inchon means "Hi, there" in Chinese.

And Pork Chop Hill is a farm in Iowa.

Perhaps he believes the 38th parallel is something left over from his high school geometry class.

Layered between World War II and Vietnam, Korea somehow never earned the definition as a hot item in American history.

The mud and misery of Korea's three years lay in an obscure corner of the young man's storehouse of historical knowledge. I'm not sure my friend was entirely certain who fought in Korea. Or when.

I suspect he did not know why, but I forgive him for that because many people who were there are still trying to figure that one out.

The conflict has been called America's forgotten war. I never really believed that, but I'm beginning to.

A recent poll showed that many young M*A*S*H* fans think the setting of that entertainment is World War II or the Vietnam War.

Not so. If the Korean War's immortality rests with the memory of its veterans, then it certainly is destined to slip closer to nothingness before too many more years have passed. The men and women who served there are beginning to nudge the other side of middle age.

Layered between World War II and Vietnam, Korea somehow never earned the definition as a hot item in American history.

World War II ended a madness so perverse we are all still trying to comprehend it. The Vietnam War killed a portion of this nation's population, and it seriously wounded the rest of it.

So the accounts of those two conflicts will persevere. But the Korean War sort of just sits there. It rests quietly on a few pages of history books.

Death, though, dealt just as thoroughly with the soldiers in the cold of Korea as it did with those who died in the heat of Vietnamese jungles.

The most current World Almanac puts the battle death toll in Korea at 33,629 Americans in the years between 1950 and 1953. The same book lists 47,356 U.S. battle deaths in the 11 years between 1964 and 1973 in Vietnam.

About 11,200 GIs died per year in Korea, more than twice the number who were killed annually in South Vietnam.

Yet the memory betrays many. But not all.

I shared lunch not long ago with some guys who remember very well. They all were members of the 224th Infantry Regiment of the California National Guard's 40th Division.

The regiment was activated in Ontario 42 years ago last week, and was shipped out to Camp Cook. Most of the regiment saw combat before the Korean War's end.

The guys I lunched with gather every couple of months. They meet at the Iron Skillet in Ontario, which, ironically enough, is owned by Steve Teng, who is Chinese but was born in Seoul.

These old soldiers—sometimes as many as 30 of them—convene not to deal in war stories, but to enjoy life and one another.

Bob Ellingwood was there. He was the young duty officer who received the call for the regiment to pack up that September day in 1950. And there were Ollie Hickman, Vern Kruggel, Laird Hudson, Chuck Chapman, Don Seely, Jim Godwin and Rex Melendrez. And others were present.

They came from throughout the Inland Valley and beyond. They ranged in rank from colonel to grunts and ground pounders.

But now they all are part of a uncomplicated camaraderie that was wrought in another time.

And they all belong to a little legion that won't forget.

Dorothy Grant

Attempting to describe the goodness of Dorothy Grant is like trying to tell someone what's so pretty about the sea at sundown.

It's difficult to abbreviate the wonder of it.

Something like trying to explain to a child why you cry at weddings when everyone else is so happy. You just do, that's why.

Dorothy is so full of good that defining her unselfishness is like trying to tell someone why you love your mother.

Dorothy's magnificence is simple, but it challenges simple definition. It would be like explaining what you believe Mary of *The Pieta* is thinking.

And like *The Pieta's* mother, Dorothy grieves. She is, among other things, a mother to a whole town.

"I don't deal in color, I deal in people. When I look at you now I don't see white, I see a man."

The have-nots are her children. The sick are to be held. The troubled listened to. The hungry fed. The ragged clothed. And those with dreams of better things encouraged.

For about the past 15 years she has been a community volunteer. But it's more than that. It seems that Dorothy is omnipresent. She is everywhere that people need help, but much of the time she can be found at the Jesse Turner Center in North Fontana.

She raises funds for any project in town that will help someone out. She constantly seeks donations of clothing, food, and toys.

Dorothy sees to the distribution of food bank items to 2,000 low-income people per month. And she is a tough and aggressive fund-raiser.

"I'll take money from anywhere," she said, "even if it comes from Little Hat, Australia, and I don't even know if there is such a place."

And she provides scholarships to students with proceeds from a snack bar she operates at the Turner Center.

Dorothy still has close ties with the schools where she worked for many years, and when there is trouble on campus she is sometimes called to help quiet things down even before the police are summoned.

She drives sick people to the doctor, the hospital or wherever, even if it's in Los Angeles. She is not paid.

She sleeps only about four hours a night, but never misses church.

Dorothy quilts and sells her work for the only money that goes directly to her, and she uses it to help pay for her transportation of the sick and needy or others who need a lift. All other money she raises goes directly to the Turner Center or other beneficiaries.

She is well known for getting things done that need to be done. Standing outside the center she pointed across the grounds and said, "They were slow getting the lawn in up there by the picnic shelter, so I went down to City Hall and raised hell. Got the grass, too," she said with a snapping nod.

Before she retired, she worked for 24 years with the Fontana Unified School District.

When asked how old she is she clipped, "I'm a senior."

Then, "At one time I knew everyone in town, but no more. It's changed too much." Everyone in Fontana knows her, though. She was born in Louisiana. Her father was a teacher and a red cap for the railroad. Her mother died when Dorothy was a child.

She spoke proudly of her father. "He was part Shawhnee," she said, "and was a good teacher."

Dorothy, who is black, said "I was raised up in a white home after my parents were gone."

Asked if she works mostly with the black community Dorothy simply said, "I don't deal in color, I deal in people. When I look at you now I don't see white, I see a man."

Not long ago her 1976 Nova broke down after Dorothy drove a woman to a Los Angeles hospital.

"I don't know if the old car will make it," she said. "It's in the shop and they haven't told me yet. I'm hoping some day I can buy a little truck to haul donated goods around in."

"That's what I'm hoping and praying for. A little truck."

Helpless

Sitting atop an idle basketball, my neighbor Schumway watched me at work.

It was last fall, and we were on the patio. I was attempting to find health in a outdoor light that had been flickering with some sort of weird electronic malaise.

We decided it had become moribund, and if I couldn't reverse the course of things by producing a quick remedy, the light surely would go out forever.

What I did not realize at the time was I simply was passing time while my wife was in the house calling the electrician.

When I learned help was on the way, ol' Schumway and I went inside to watch a little fast break.

My wife called me "Sparky" for awhile—at least until the bandages came off.

My ineptitude concerning anything that requires repair or dexterous attention is well known in our home—and the neighborhood.

I am, according by virtually universal assessment, not handy.

A neighbor once said I was the only person he knows who can foul up a full-size anvil.

I broke a golf ball once.

I called on Chuck Radney across the street one day, and when he answered the front door he saw me standing on the porch with a screwdriver in my hand. "Put it down," he said quickly, and with alarm, "you'll hurt yourself."

An electrician (it might have been the same one who finally fixed the patio light) was called once to complete a project I had undertaken in the kitchen.

I had been trying to mend a wall plug. The electrician told my wife, in my absence of course, "Your husband had the right idea. But I think he knows just enough to be dangerous."

I wondered later how he could discern my weakness by just looking at my work.

Some time ago I was tending to a light switch in the hallway when something went *zzzzt!*

That sucker sparked me—sort of went off in my hand. I was slightly burned.

I said a couple of words that cannot be found in the electrician's how-to manual, and my wife scolded me for committing a bit of blasphemy.

"It was just a quick prayer," I said. "I was scared."

My wife called me "Sparky" for awhile—at least until the bandages came off.

Schumway is similarly afflicted. Once when attempting to fix his garage door opener, he locked himself in there over night while his nice wife was on a trip.

I've never done that.

He and I, years ago, often undertook repair projects as a team. My wife ultimately dissolved that partnership fearing that someday we would blow up the house.

We repaired a hallway light once, but when the job was complete we discovered that the switch controlling the light wound up indicating the light was "on" when it was "off," and "off" when it was "on."

Our family became accustomed to the idiosyncrasy, but the condition confused our house guests.

Schumway and I brought normal function back to a front porch light once, but when we were finished we learned the light was permanently illuminated.

It didn't seem to matter whether the switch was on or not.

My wife called the electrician several days later when the light bulb gave out.

There have been many times I have begun repair efforts only to have them completed by understanding and helpful neighbors such as Chuck, George Trentz or Charlie Sather.

I would call on their help alternately in the attempt to avoid wearing out a good thing.

Those guys are nimble with their hands. And their heads work. One of them once questioned the normalcy of my own hands and head. Oh, well.

All this leads to the explanation of why last Christmas I received a gift that must be recorded right up there with the most unusual but practical of all time.

It was a personalized copy of the Yellow Pages.

It was my wife's idea. But Chuck, Charlie and George helped with the gift wrapping.

The Barber Shop

The barber shop I regularly visit is, among other things, a cradle of information.

The place is small, but it serves as a faithful tributary to my reservoir of knowledge.

I have come to learn there, for example, Gene Autry's wife should never have let Wally Joyner leave the Angels, and motorists on the San Bernardino Freeway don't always use all five fingers when they wave at one another.

And you can hear nearly four in a row on KFROG while waiting to get through the Mission Boulevard traffic lights on any given Friday afternoon.

And that's a lot of country music.

I was in the barber shop some time ago when the guy sitting next to me abruptly learned something himself.

During the course of jaunty conversation, the fellow took a whack at using the word, "hyperbole."

"That word doesn't rhyme with diaper bowl," Jim Stinson corrected him, not even looking up from his clippers where he was working on Roy Bryant.

So much for the English lesson.

The good old days occupy a space in time supended somewhere between myth, real and want.

On another day in that tonsorial palace the guys agreed that the most popular topic of conversation in the good old days was—and get this—the good old days.

It means good times are never now. They are more like a mirage that is chasing us—a shimmering image of imagined comfort lying in the past.

The good old days occupy a space in time suspended somewhere between myth, real and want.

Perhaps some of the most wretched days of this century fell during the Great Depression, yet we often hear some survivors of that misery refer to it as "the good old days."

Why? People of that time were occupied with priorities in which human despair, values and personal relationships were tested on righteous ground.

They often did not look much beyond the beginning of tomorrow. But they had one another.

As historian James Shelton wrote of that era, "No matter how bad things were, by pulling together we would somehow come out of it together and alive."

Inland Valley residents of that time were a hearty, farming lot who exemplified that survival.

Ask Art Bridge, Walter Stewart, Dick DuVall or Bert Francis—they know.

World War II, which later washed across the entire globe in hideous fashion, provided a sense of communal gratification to those who made it through and helped bring some sense of order back to a crazy world.

"The Good War" it was later to be called.

Other generations also experienced their own brand of good old days, even if those people had to wait until that time had passed to enjoy it.

There is much that is not right in our valley, state, nation and world today. But there is a lot that is right about it, too.

Perhaps some day these times will come to be judged as "good."

That may be difficult for us contemporaries to imagine, but a bit of truth may hang somewhere in the mirage.

Most people are pulling together so we can somehow come out of it together and alive. But some will not make it, and they will be the victims of our time, not the survivors of it. Sad.

Not too long ago I visited the barber shop with a companion who was an out-of-town guest in our home. He was, years ago, a frequent and youthful visitor to the shop.

The banter that day followed a familiar pace.

There were some laughs. Ed Smothers, at the No. 1 chair, presided in his unique manner.

The customers nor the barbers seemed to take themselves, each other, or events, too seriously. Except the Wally Joyner thing.

It was a warm encounter. When my companion and I left the shop, he said to me, "What a neat experience."

"What do you mean?" I asked.

"Being in there is just like going back to the good old days," he said.

I just smiled.

I looked back at the shop, and for a second I thought I saw it shimmer a bit.

Like a mirage.

The Quakes

The man I was talking to was big. Like an oak tree.

When we shook hands mine went out of sight. But he was gentle, too.

We stood in the sun and talked about the way people in the valley seem to be immersed in some sort of wondrous and wacky adoration for 25 young men who call themselves the Quakes.

Then the big man said, "That standing ovation they were given at the end of the opening game almost brought tears to my eyes." Translation: "That standing ovation they were given at the end of the opening game BROUGHT tears to my eyes."

He is that kind of man, and it was that kind of opening.

They'd rather play baseball than eat, and their dreams are bigger than all of right field.

The ovation my friend talked about was not a raucous cheer. The fans simply rose and stood with dignified applause that rolled out across the whole ballpark.

The young men of swat, slam and eternal hope accepted the tribute as they left the field following the tribal rite of victory at the mound.

The applause was full of grace. Rich and somber.

For weeks I have worked to understand the affection for the Rancho Cucamonga Quakes. It is, I thought, a challenging phenomenon to define—like trying to grab a feather in the wind.

Who are those guys? Why do we stand and cheer? Why do we have lumps in our throats?

The Quakes are a Class A minor league baseball team. A group of down-home boys who are no older than about 22. Most of them weren't born when Nolan Ryan threw his first professional smoke through the strike zone.

They are no-names who ride a bus when the team is on the road. They don't make enough money to have homes, so small groups of them put their money together and rent apartments.

Thus the Quakes' double-play combination could read: Dishwasher to Cook to Housekeeper. The real combination is Drinkwater to Hartke to Pugh.

They'd rather play baseball than eat, and their dreams are bigger than all of right field.

They're everybody's son, or brother, or uncle. Or maybe even sweetheart. And if you yield to it, the Walter Mitty will stir inside you, and you become a Quake yourself.

Those young people have looked beyond the rim of things, and have seen adventures the rest of us only read about.

I learned something of them the other day as I sat in the dugout during batting practice talking to the first baseman. He is Scott Pugh, a West Texan who tried to pick up his first T-ball bat when it was longer than he was.

He has wanted to play baseball since he could talk. The only thing he wants more is to be a high school baseball coach and history teacher when his pro days are over. He'll make it.

His dad is a trucking company executive in Abilene, and his mother teaches high school there. Both of them were in the Quakes' stands over the weekend.

Scott's high school sweetheart, Kristin, is waiting for him in Abilene where she is studying to be a teacher. And trust me, she's waiting for a gentleman.

Meanwhile, Scott cut himself a piece of history last Thursday when he hit the first home run ever at Rancho Cucamonga Stadium, making him kind of the Neil Armstrong of the right-field fence.

But most of all, I learned that Scott and the rest of the Quakes do what they do because they're having so much fun. "I'm very lucky to be able to play this game every day," Scott told me.

And goals? "I set my goals one day at a time, and right now it is to come out here and have a good time."

And as he does, he pulls the rest of us along with him while he plays the game. He does it in such away that we forget what was bothering us earlier in the day. Or yesterday. Or last week.

It allows us to look beyond the rim of things.

And that, I think, is why we stand and cheer.

The Shoes

The perception I have of my grandfather is a narrow one.

Why? Because it was created in the mind of a child. I knew him from the time Mother Nature gave me memory until I was in my 12th year when the old man died.

The first emotion I can recall regarding my relationship with my father's father was stark fear. He was not mean, but in those early years I didn't know any better, and I thought he was.

I cannot say there ever was a loving bond between us, but my state of fright diminished with time. I finally just regarded him as stern.

He never referred to me by my name, choosing to call me "kid." I was annoyed by that, because when he used the word it always gave the conversation a certain ring of scold to it.

He was, however, a quiet man, choosing to speak only when he judged there was purpose in it.

He was old, and I thought he probably always had been. His daily attire included a shirt, tie and suspenders—even at family picnics.

He was tall, straight and thin. His bald head and his age gave him a skullish look, and his deep-set and dark eyes were piercing and, to me, menacing.

"You just couldn't keep your hands off that, could you, kid!" he might have said when catching me holding a piece from his precious collection of tiny and delicate figurines.

By the definition of some folk, my grandfather was profane. "Damn" and "hell" were regularly used portions of his vocabulary. And "God damn" was not uncommon in his speech. He never used foul language.

He was a religious man, and he did not regard the use of his words as any sort of blasphemy. To him they were just adjectives.

He was a devoted St. Louis Cardinals fan, and listened to their games regularly.

Sometimes he would talk back to the radio. Such as, "The God damn umpire must be blind, that guy was safe by a God damn mile!"

If the runner played for the Chicago Cubs he was, of course, out by a similar distance.

The talk was tolerated by my grandmother. My mother was always annoyed by it, and my father, having grown up around such speech, thought it was normal.

In keeping with his quiet way, my grandfather never talked much about himself. But others did, and their stories about him were numerous. Here's one:

As a relatively young widower, he courted an old-maid school teacher some years after his wife died. The courtship took place long before I was born. The teacher later became a dear grandmother to me because I never had a real one of my own.

She taught 14 ragamuffin children in a one-room schoolhouse out in the country. The children were farm dwellers whose parents tried to wring profit from tough dirt in difficult times.

Not many of the students had shoes.

One day my grandfather took time out from his office in town to call on my grandmother-to-be at the schoolhouse. They stole a few minutes while the barefoot students recessed.

A few days after the visit, the man who owned the department store in town showed up at the school with 14 pairs of shoes. They already had been paid for, the merchant said.

My grandfather never mentioned the incident. Ever. And those who knew him best did not consider asking him about it. No need. The truth was just sort of there.

But a mystery forever remained, at least to me: Why did all the shoes fit; and why was there a proper number of shoes for girls as well as boys?

Who knows?

Many years later my grandfather died, and his passing was my first experience with death in the family. My old one-time nemesis was gone.

I cried.

And the older I become, the greater understanding I have of why I did.

Shopping Quietly

There is a young member of our family whose birthday falls precisely one month after December 25.

That festive occasion evolves into something of a bumper crop of Yuletide joy for her each year. Sort of Christmas revisited.

She collects a number of presents similar to what she receives in December, but the red and green decor of that season give way to more conventional colors.

Her birthday, of course, renews the need for the rest of us to shop for presents.

Settling on what gifts are proper for girls and women has always challenged my judgment and good sense.

Having grown up with no sisters, and fathered only sons, my knowledge of just what type of presents appeal to women is critically lacking.

> *The clerk looked at it for a moment, then lifted her head. She had the kindest eyes I've ever seen.*

Shopping for my mother had seemed easy enough, but buying for other women has always been vexing.

I fear I will botch it somehow by giving them something too personal, too feminine, not feminine enough, or something only a man would appreciate.

Power tools are out.

I sought help from my wife, asking her what I might purchase for the January birth child.

"Why not a fragrance of some kind?" she said. "A nice cologne, perfume, eau de toilette or something?"

She mentioned a particular scent, the label of which was in the French.

The language element could be trouble, I thought.

"How can I possibly buy something I can't even pronounce?" I asked her. "Here, write it down," she said, handing me a slip of paper.

She spelled it out for me and I jotted it down on the paper.

"Just hand it to the saleslady, she'll know what it means," my wife said.

When the time was right for me to make the purchase, I was, by no particular design, in a strange town in a strange store.

I wished I could have talked to Cheryl Garcia, who lives in San Dimas and nurtures shoppers of fragrance at Nordstrom's in Montclair. She has helped me before. But I wasn't in Montclair.

With questionable courage, I walked up to a clerk at a counter where an abundance of aroma was for sale.

I set down the slip of paper on which I had written the French word that described the cologne I was to purchase.

The clerk looked at it for a moment, then lifted her head. She had the kindest eyes I've ever seen. Then quietly she wrote on a piece of her own paper, "What price range are you interested in?"

Obviously this extremely nice and thoughtful person assumed I was unable to speak, very possibly unable to hear. Her compassion and sensitivity were touching.

What to do? I was reluctant to speak, because I was fearful of embarrassing her. I didn't want that.

I turned the piece of paper around and wrote, "Some size in a mid-price range would be fine."

She removed a container from the case, set it before me and inscribed the price on the piece of paper, which we were, by now, sharing.

YIKES, I nearly blurted out, not realizing how much the price of good smell had escalated since I last bought perfume.

My "yikes" exclamation would have ruined everything and shattered our silent world. But the gods were with me, and instead of speaking, I returned to the pencil and asked to see a smaller size.

Finally, I decided on a sensible amount. The scent was especially beckoning.

"I'll take it," I wrote.

"Would you like it gift wrapped?" came the written response.

We were on a third piece of paper by now.

I just nodded. And smiled.

When she gave me the handsome package, she took the extra time to write, "Have a nice day."

I drew a happy face on the piece of paper and wished her well, too.

Later, I proudly announced to my wife that I had found the French scent.

"How did the slip of paper work?" she asked. "What did the clerk say when you handed it to her?"

"Actually, she didn't say much at all," I responded, figuring it would be best to leave it at that.

Old Dogs And Childern

I was driving around the valley the other day when I saw a child playing in the sparkle of a world on its way to an early spring.

The morning sun brushed her blond hair, making it look as if it had been kissed by the goddess in charge of making little girls pretty.

The child's state of glee—if it could have been shared across the land—would have made the whole world happy.

Her bright eyes were a portion of a smile that was so wide it looked as if it could survive but a moment before becoming downright laughter.

She was alone and standing still at the corner of a tired house hoping the adversary in her game of hide and seek would not find her. At least not soon.

I was caught up in the little hider's anticipation, and my heart pulsed along with hers.

Although we are not all created equal, we are all born innocent.

For I could see the other player in the game, although neither of them could see one another. A meeting of the two was a certainty, and it was imminent.

I had to drive on before it happened, but I could envision the eruption that would come with the two girls' sure-to-be-sharp encounter I knew there would be an explosion of excitement. A song of joy.

The girls played in a poor neighborhood.

Peel had come to the paint.

A sagging car occupied the front yard.

So did an old couch.

There was poverty here, all right but it did not invade the girls' bliss and peace in the sun. The children were happy in that springtime instant.

A few days later I was at the edge of the sea looking out across the shore that had been washed by an all-night rain.

The earth and sky were clean, and I felt that if someone were to let me stand on his shoulders I could have seen all the way to China.

I decided to go into a little church nearby. Its tidy grounds beside the surf were shaded by giant eucalyptus trees.

A young priest inside spoke not in sermon but more in religious soliloquy.

"All men," he said quietly, "are not created equal."

I pondered the statement and reflected on it later.

And I thought of the little girls playing hide and seek in a yard without lawn.

There is, I thought, a certain unfairness in the American promise that equality comes with birth.

It's not something you can count on.

The priest was right, people are not created equal—not even with equal opportunity.

Not all of us can stay in the air as long as Michael Jordan does.

Not all of us can save the whole world the way Winston Churchill's leadership did.

We can't all live in a house on a hill.

We cannot all sing.

You even have to work hard at the U.S. Army commercial's invitation to "Be all that you can be!"

I do not question the valor and value of the men whose Declaration of Independence proclaimed that all men are created equal and who promised better things for those who were to follow them into history.

But still there are tests in this life we all must true up to. And among them is the fact that we are not equal in every way, and are not all traveling on an uninterrupted track to the Good Life.

What is true, however, is that although we are not all created equal, we are all born innocent.

I thought of the little girls again. And of their innocence and how truth and innocence are so tightly bound.

The children, I thought, are not yet corrupted by those willing to teach corruption.

Then I recalled the words of the country song:

Old dogs

And children

And watermelon wine

Unpretentious.

Innocent. Fragile and fleeting.

A Favor For Mah Wong

Mah Wong knew he was going to die. Soon.

He was 87, and not long before, he had watched his little shack burn down. Not much was left for him now, he thought.

The ashes of his home matched his own fragile hold on life.

His family was gone, and so were the rest of those in the Chinese settlement that had been his whole world for so many years.

Mah Wong's friends had gradually moved away, choosing to join a modern world that was leaving the little settlement hurrying into history.

He was left behind, caught somewhere between yesterday and tomorrow. He was the last. It's over, he must have said to himself.

> *He was left behind, caught somewhere between yesterday and tomorrow.*

So Mah Wong went up to Louella's place to ask a favor. He had offered her plenty of help in the past, he reasoned, so now would be a good time to ask a favor in return.

Surely Louella would remember the times he helped her around the house—the yard work, laundry and other chores. He even cared for the children.

Louella Wangler lived in Cucamonga, and was among many of the neighbors who had a special love for Mah Wong.

That's why she and others helped him in any way they could after the flames brought frightful wreckage to his life.

Louella remembered Mah Wong's earlier years, and the times when the Chinese settlement was first called Chinatown or China House.

It was home to several families who worked the vineyards and the groves that spread out south from the mountains.

Mah Wong thought of those lively days as he shuffled to Louella's house on his hunt for the favor. He carried a small paper bag with him.

When he was younger his people filled a dozen houses along San Bernardino Road not far from the Klusman Ranch.

All the buildings were attached. Perhaps that's why some people called the place China House.

Those were good times, Mah Wong was thinking—a hard day's work followed by the certain daily bath, a meal of fish and rice, and then the

31

joy of a good clay pipe.

He remembered listening to the old men, some who could remember stories of the railroad building and the gold rush up north.

Those days, Mah Wong was told, were not so good. White American settlers, miners and ranch hands feared the presence of the Chinese because their hard work threatened the settlers' jobs.

But times were better here in the south. Better, that is, before the young people began to leave Cucamonga's Chinatown. Especially better before another and earlier fire destroyed a large part of the entire settlement.

Mah Wong thought of that tragedy and it reminded him of his own more recent bad luck.

He remembered old On Toy, Chinatown's boss. On Toy returned to his native China every few years to visit his wives, and sometimes he would return with one of his sons. He was not allowed to bring a wife with him to California.

When On Toy returned to Cucamonga the men in the settlement enjoyed hearing of his adventures in Canton.

Mah Wong thought of those stories on his way to Louella's.

When he arrived at her home he showed her the contents of his little paper bag—tiny bits of confetti-like material cut from newspapers.

He wanted, he said, to ask a favor of his old friend. Mah Wong told Louella that he was getting old and said, "Please, when I die, sprinkle these pieces of paper around me to keep the Devil away."

He died a short time later, and Louella and a friend took his body to San Bernardino where Mah Wong was buried in a public plot.

That was in 1939.

When the mourners left the grave the little pieces of paper began to scatter and blow away in the wind.

And Mah Wong slipped into history with the rest of Cucamonga's Chinatown and was gone forever.

Dorothy Wisely

The snowflakes were so large that they soon covered the canyon in huge soft drifts, bringing a great stillness to the mountain.

Those outside could scarcely hear a sound, and those inside moved closer to whatever was warm.

It was December 17, nearly 46 years ago, and the kids were busy in Mt. Baldy's one-room schoolhouse where glee and gladness brought their own brand of warmth to the little building.

The less-than-30 pupils were working to plane down the roughness of their Christmas program.

The students—grades one through—six had only one teacher, and the kids called her "Miz Fagg," as if she didn't have a first name at all.

Her whole name was Dorothy Fagg and she was pleased with the progress of the holiday program rehearsal.

> *The students listened as if God were talking to them.*

There was a knock at the schoolhouse door, and the storm gave up one Allden Wisely, who was there to visit his nephew. The boy was one of Miz Fagg's students.

Al looked like the mountain itself. Bits of snow clung to his cap although he had brushed himself off outside.

"He was dressed in his ski clothes and he had quite a presence about him," Dorothy said later.

Al told the kids stories of his skiing on the steep slopes higher up the mountain, and the students listened as if God were talking to them.

Dorothy and Al never had met before that day. But they wed nine years later—"We didn't exactly run off and get married," she said.

Then they spent their lives together in a house Al built for Dorothy with his own hands. The house is still there. So is Dorothy.

Al died in 1984 after spending 56 of his 75 years in the Village working as a carpenter, builder and jack-of-all-trades. He moved to the canyon in 1928.

I visited Dorothy the other day. Her home is as gracious as she is. It's on the main road next to the ranger station.

The house is shaped and painted like an old red barn. A totem pole stands at attention in the front yard.

Inside, the home is like a grandmother's house. Warm. Comforting.

Visiting with Dorothy Wisely is like reading a book of another time. She was the last to serve as the only teacher of Mt. Baldy's one-room school house.

She has lived in the village for nearly 60 years, so I asked if she has been there longer than anyone else. "Oh, no. There's at least Bill Sager, owner of the Buckhorn; Bob Bentley and Bobby Chapman, of the Chapman Ranch. Bobby was born here in about 1927."

She told me of early-day toll roads, mining camps, floods, and a hunter named Fred Dell, who built what might have been the first couple of cabins in the canyon. He put them up in 1886 where the trout pools are now.

Then there was Charles Baynahm, who built the first lodge (Buckhorn now) in about 1906 and called it "Camp Baynahm Hotel." The entire community came to be called "Camp Baynahm."

That name survived until the ownership of the lodge changed hands, then the village was named "Camp Baldy." It kept that name until the early 1950s when villagers petitioned to rename it "Mt. Baldy."

The original one-room Camp Baldy school was abandoned and the new and present school of eight grades was dedicated in 1976.

One of Dorothy's many interests now is helping raise funds to restore the original schoolhouse where she taught. She hopes the project will be complete by sometime next spring.

Meanwhile, she goes on loving the mountain and the people who live there. And thinking of that snowy day 46 years ago.

If the restored schoolhouse is dedicated on June 10 next year, the celebration will have special meaning for Dorothy. It's her birthday.

She will be 84.

Dako

Dako's smile is as kind as a gentle touch. The grin puts a squint in his eyes in such a way that you want to smile along with him. So you do.

His eyes sparkle. Like Johnny Mathis'.

Dako is small. He is incredibly handsome. He is dressed a bit baggy, but he's neat as well as polite in conversation.

He is 17.

My first question to him was, "Dako, what makes you do graffiti? What is there to it?"

He smiled again. "It's mobbing, getting up. You gotta write with style. Your gotta get fame so you can get into a crew."

"How do you get fame?"

"The more you write, the more fame you get. You gotta mob or write—get your tag up (plaster a jillion walls and signs with graffiti). When you get fame, you can get into a crew. You gotta get your tag up."

Our talk went on:

Q.—Are crews street gangs?

A.—No, you don't have to get jumped to get into a crew (be beaten by at least four gang members). You just gotta get fame, do a lot of writing. Go mobbing. Get your tag up. We're not gangs. Instead of fighting like gangs do, we have spray fights. The crew who puts up the most tags during a spree wins.

Q.—How many crews are in a local city, say like Ontario?

A.—About 10. Some have only a few writers in them. The one I'm in has about 80. I'm one of the leaders.

Q.—Can you be a gang member and a member of a crew at the same time?

A.— No. Never.

Q.—How long have you been writing?

A.—Since I was about 12 or 13.

> "Everyone in the crew hangs around with each other. It's like a family. We're always together."

Q.—Do gang members leave you alone or do they bother you?

A.—Older members, deep into gangs, know the difference between gangs and crews. But some of the younger gangsters might want to punk us up (harass us) sometimes.

Q.—Are there any crew members who are girls?

A.—There are about 15 or so girls in my crew. The rest are made up of every size, color and shape—Mexicans, blacks, white, Asians, Puerto Ricans—everyone.

Q.—How old are the writers?

A.—From about 12 to 18.

Q.—Do you realize how much it costs to clean up graffiti?

A.—We really don't care, but we know how much it costs. What we are doing is no worse than what other people did when they were young. We know it makes people mad. No one can say they were always good and paid attention to all the rules.
We just feel we have to do something bad. You'll never get rid of graffiti. It will always be here. The best thing cities can do is give writers cleanup time (make them remove their own graffiti). We don't mind that.

Q.—Do you write because you don't like someone or you feel you and your neighbors aren't treated right?

A.—There ain't no protest to it. It has nothing to do with City Hall, the cops, school or rich people. We're not against anything. I, myself, am dedicated to graffiti. It's an urge. Writers who get into crews then give it up are not really dedicated.

Q.—Does your mother know you're a writer?

A.—Yes. When I was first picked up (Dako has been arrested for tagging about 15 times) they called her to the police department to pick me up. She grounded me for about a week. Now she just picks me up at the police station, and we go home.
You can't tell a writer to stop just like that. You're addicted to writing. Once it starts it's like you can't stop. (Because tagging is a misdemeanor, and in view of crowded courts and juvenile halls, police told me they have little option other than to release taggers to their parents.)

Q.—Did you ever want to quit?

A.—Yes, a long time ago.

Q.—Why?

A.—Because I've thought about jail. I would miss things I see on the street everyday. I would miss seeing my friends. Being in one room would make a person go crazy. I can't stay in one place. I've gotta move. But graffiti is my life right now. I'm dedicated to it.

Q.—Where do you buy your paint?

A.—A good writer racks (steals) his own paint. A good writer can rack 15 cans of spray paint in a few seconds. There's writers that will rack anything—clothing, hats, bikes, cars.

(Dako said about half of the people in crews are involved in other crimes in some way, but that activity has nothing to do with graffiti or tagging or getting "fame.")

Q.—Do crews ever hold meetings?

A.—Oh, yeah. We meet every month or so. Sometimes we have a barbecue. We rack everything—the meat, sauce, everything. At the meetings we tell whoever isn't getting their tag up, to get it up or get out. We tell them what to hit. And some new writers coming up now show disrespect by writing on houses and private businesses. We tell the new guys coming up to knock off the disrespect. Good writers just tag main streets, freeways and abandoned buildings.

Q.—How much writing can you do in a single night?

A.—You write until you run out of paint. During a spree that lasts all night, three to five writers will use 100 cans. If I'm on a spree I don't let anything get in my way. You get more fame for dangerous writing, like freeway signs that don't have a walkway underneath.

Q.—What do the tags mean?

A.—Every writer has his own name. Like mine is Dako. It can be two letters or more. And we have numbers, too. Mine is 447. (Dako's name and number have been changed for this account.) And the crew has a three-letter name. Those are the tags. The more we put up, the more fame we will have.

Q.—Do you go to school?

A.—No. I was expelled for fighting with a gang member, and I am on probation for trespassing. But I have never been in jail. I can't get back in school, so I feel I am denied that. But that gives me more time for writing.

Q.—Would you want your little brother to become a writer?

A.—No. I wouldn't want the cops to look at him the way they look at me.

Then I asked Dako when he last went on a spree.

"I haven't written for a while. On vacation, I guess. But I will write again. That's all we know is to mob, tag and get up.

"You're not anybody if you're not in a crew or a gang. Everyone in the crew hangs around with each other. It's like a family. We're always together."

"When do you think you might go writing again?" I asked.

" Who knows, I might go tonight."

Big Ol' Virgil

My propensity to conform often rises to almost pathological dimension.

I follow directions, do what I'm told. Abide by the rules. Be a good citizen. If the sign says, "Form Two Lines," I try my best to do it, even if I'm alone.

The day I got my driver's license I rolled through a stop sign, so I went down to the police station in our little town and turned myself in. Roy, the nice old chief, told me to forget it. "Just don't do it again."

If the sign says, "Honk if You Like Garth Brooks," I honk. It would seem wrong not to.

I take a number at Claro's Italian Market even if I'm the only customer in there, simply because the sign says, "Please Take a Number."

After returning from the grocery store the other day, I discovered I had gone through the 10-item express lane with 11 items.

As the big guy left, Schumway said, "I think that guy's nuts."

"What'll I do?" I asked my wife. "I'd better take the crackers back."

"Please don't do that."

"I at least could go over and apologize to the checker—maybe even to the manager."

"Don't do that either."

Some time ago my ol' buddy and neighbor, Schumway, and I were fishing on a small lake in the High Sierra. We had left our wives and kids behind and were doing a little angling on our own.

We had just settled down. Ol' Schumway was sitting on his ice chest of Colorado Kool Aid, bait in the water. I was fumbling around putting salmon eggs on my treble hook.

"Hey, here comes a big ol' guy," Schumway said. I looked up and saw a huge man coming down the trail.

"He must be eight feet tall," Schumway said quietly. "And look at that star on his shirt. I'll bet his name's Virgil."

"Howdy, boys. Name's Virgil Bowman of the Bear Mountain Fire District. How's it going?"

He didn't have a uniform on, just that star on his shirt.

"Fine. Got our licenses and everything," I said, with good citizenship throbbing in my breast I hoped that would please him. Boy was he ever big.

"But have you got an ax and bucket?" Schumway and I looked at each other. The blankness on my friend's face was absolute.

"No, but we've got plenty of Velveeta and marshmallows," Schumway said with a crooked smile.

"Gotta have an ax and bucket. Never know when you might run into a wild fire. It's district law."

"One bucket sure would make a short brigade," Schumway said.

"C'mon, Schum," I whispered. "Don't tick him off."

"Fifty dollar fine if you don't have an ax and bucket. But I'll tell you what, I'll just give you boys this li'l ol' warnin' note. But you'd better get an ax and bucket before tomorrow. There's a store just down the road that sells 'em."

"Right, your honor, ah, I mean officer," I said.

As the big guy left, Schumway said, "I think that guy's nuts."

"Can't be. He's the law. Didn't you see that badge?"

When we got to the store a real nice lady clerk sold us the necessary equipment. It looked more like a hatchet and a pail.

"That'll be $30," she said.

"Isn't that kinda high?"

"It's official, though."

As we were leaving the little store we noticed ol' Virgil come in the back way and give the clerk a big hug and a kiss.

"You know what I think? I think Virgil owns this store," Schumway said "And I think the clerk is Mrs. Virgil. That's what I think. We've been conned."

"It's the law. Can't go against the law," I said, good citizenship stirring again.

"The law my six-pack, he's just an 8-foot-tall guy who owns a store and is hanging two-bit axes and buckets on suckers like us."

"Let's just get out of here," I said.

The last time I saw the bucket, months later, Schumway's daughter was making a castle with it in the sand at San Clemente.

I kept the hatchet, though. Never know when I might encounter Virgil again.

And if I do I'll only have to buy a bucket.

Running Through The Night

Before the storm growled to its greatest fury last week taking with it life and chattel, some concern was given to a lesser threat — one that could harm the valley's crops.

Like, "Do you think the rain will hurt the rhubarb?"

During that time a news writer came to me in search of a contact with a citrus grower. Did I know of anyone who still owns groves? asked the reporter.

The writer's mission, of course, was to assess the health—or lack there of—of the trees, and the buds and fruit to come.

Had the storm caused damage?

As I sought to help him, names of citrus ranchers and their families flashed through my mind.

I began to realize in an unhappy instant that many of these people were gone, retired, or through some other manner were lost from the hold of memory.

Another remnant of the long night was the pots' smoke that hovered over the valley and replaced the sky.

The Wheelers, Latimers, Stewarts, Lucases, Showalters and others are all clans long separated from those vibrant times.

Most of the trees are little more than history now. My colleague's voice seemed to fade and become echoed as my mind wandered backward.

I felt I was slipping into a weird sort of flashback where sounds and images seemed to become reflections in a tranquil pond that has been lightly disturbed.

The reverie was like a walk in another time. I could see those orange and lemon groves extending as far south as Holt Boulevard where there is nothing but houses and commerce now.

Looking down from northern elevations, one could see only a giant green carpet. The groves rolled out and turned east through Redlands and Riverside.

In our own valley there was nothing much north of Foothill Boulevard other in those ordered groves and assorted ranch houses fashioned from river rock.

Citrus was king.

There was scarcely a valley resident who was not touched in some way by the economy of the fruit.

This juicy gold was just a portion of the call to Plain States escapees who were running ahead of dust, wind and other wrath.

Steinbeck's Jodes were among the most notable of those refugees, although they passed through here and came to rest near Fresno where table grapes, as well citrus shared the king's crown.

Rain did little to cause serious damage to the valley's groves in those days. Cold was the real enemy. It came in the night. And it could be as hurtful as fire.

What was used to work against that chilling adversary were the old smudge pots, those oil-fed metal stoves that squatted by the thousands amid the rows of orange and lemon trees.

When fired, they would radiate heat embracing the trees in a comfortable and protecting warmth.

The pots would be lighted—one by one—in the freezing night by field workers, farmers, families of the farmers, students—anyone available if the cold was particularly deep and quick.

This army moved (sometimes on the run) through the groves, torches held at the ready in preparation to fire the next pot.

On and on through the night. In dawn's wake would be the exhausted smudgers —dirty, eyes watering, dragging themselves toward rest.

Another remnant of the long night was the pots' smoke that hovered over the valley and replaced the sky. It hung there like a levitating blackish blanket ready to settle over the whole land.

The soot of it did.

I was thinking I could smell the smudge . . .

"What about the citrus growers?" the reporter asked, pulling me back to the present.

The interruption gave me a jolt, and I felt as if someone had lifted the needle in the midst of good music.

"Look," I told the reporter. "Why don't you forget the citrus. Just call Mr. Jertberg and ask him if the rain has hurt the strawberries."

And he did.

Generation Of Vipers?

While World War II lay heaving and spent in the mid-1940s, American author Philip Wylie wrote *A Generation of Vipers*.

The book's aim was to measure the worth of those who fought, sacrificed and otherwise endured the second World War.

Wylie's work, whose title comes from Luke's Gospel, deals harshly with the author's subject. It questions the character and strength of the young people of that era who were resting from their terrible time in a global eruption that left 50 million men, women and children dead.

As in all wars, it was a youthful legion who suffered the shell, shrapnel and shock of a conflict created by those older than themselves.

Youngsters fight wars. We all know that. And Wylie wrote about these young people of the 40s.

His controversial book elevated him to a new level of chic. Today's TV talk show hosts would have wooed him.

They were, and are, a hearty lot who have always grabbed adversity by the hair.

He may not have realized it at the time, but Wylie wrote of a generation that was to become quite unlike any other of this century.

It's members survived the worst of times and enjoyed the best of times long before and long after Wylie had done his work.

Their generation was born in the first quarter of the 1900s, so most of them are in their 70s now—in the September of their lives.

They were children during the crazy 1920s and passed through their formative years during the Great Depression, the swamp of which left a signature on the generation forever.

Then came the war, which was theirs more than anyone else's. After the war they became young marrieds who went to work, or went to college on the GI Bill.

As difficult as it was, they earned their education for relatively little money. As a generation, they may be the last of the bootstrap pullers.

They lived in a time when Vaughn Monroe raced with the moon and Woody Herman played at the Woodchoppers Ball. It was after Rudy Vallee but before Elvis.

Dorsey was the King of Swing and Harry Truman was giving everyone hell. I suppose that generation had its own brand of vice. But dope and cocaine had yet to begin its chewing away at those to come.

If the depression and war had been tough on Wylie's generation, getting started in life, having children and buying homes was easy compared to what it is today.

This unique generation valued the good life as no other generation has in this century, probably because they had suffered so much creating it.

They not only scraped through the depression and withstood the war for the sake of their children, they withstood it for themselves as well.

They were, and are, a hearty lot who have always grabbed adversity by the hair.

Although I am only on the fringe of that generation, I spent the last couple of weeks with some of Wylie's people. We trundled off to Mexico and spent our days and nights on the beach of the Sea of Cortez.

Members of that generation were everywhere along the way. They enjoyed the same music, drove the same kind of RVs, and shared the same assortment of values that their time had forever left engraved on them.

And they laughed a lot. With and at themselves. They're good at that.

They are, as they always have been, a generation that appreciates what is good. They hate misery, so they stiffen against it rather than give in to it.

They are not perfect, but they are far from imperfect. They have traveled through bad and good times, and the best time for them seems to be right now.

I watched as they wore their months of September, October and November with grace and good humor.

After my travels with them I came to the conclusion that if Wylie were to view the generation of his book from this side of time, he would find no vipers there at all.

Mary And OPARC

Grief, in its normal and accepted state, can be worked on. Fought.

It's there with its frightful reality. A target. Something to overcome. A thing to strike out against and defeat.

It can be resisted as if it were a visible enemy. Although never vanquished, grief, with all its agony, can at least be reduced, and its healing progression can almost be measured.

That, they tell me, is because the usual state of grief is the result of death —a pure form of finality.

It's sort of an end to what can be a beginning for those who remain.

But I was introduced to another, not-so-normal sort of grief this week. It is not an end. Not a finality that can be left behind. It's a challenge that does not end. It's not a target to be seen and struck. It's more like a shadow.

> *"We care enough about them to let them do everything they can do for themselves,"*
> *Mary said.*

It is a grieving that begins when parents receive the devastating news that their child is developmentally disabled.

From that moment on the parents are called upon to thread their way through a new kind of life.

And there is the obvious companion problem: the life of the child.

What is to come? A monotone existence? Life in an institution? Just what?

But I found light in that world. There was great victory, courage, compassion, happiness, and a sort of caring whose meaning defies ordinary definition.

I discovered these things while visiting Mary Boyd, longtime executive director of the Association of Retarded Citizens, Ontario-Pomona, commonly called OPARC.

Mary is an angel in the company of angels who make up her staff. The guy who introduced the words "selfless" and "dedicated" to our language must have met these people first.

One arm of OPARC is a project called COPE. It is carried out by parents of children who suffer developmental disabilities. Their motto: "Can we help? We've been there . . ." These volunteers cradle and bolster parents who have just learned of their own child's disability.

"It's enormous support," Mary said. "And it works."

OPARC is best known for its operation of five work centers where the disabled can perform jobs, earn money, and find meaning to their lives.

"I have found that this is not an end for these people, but a beginning of individual growth and independence," Mary told me.

These workers, more than 200 of them, package, assemble, label, solder. And they're good at it. Their customers are large corporations, defense contractors, family-owned businesses, local governmental agencies, and much more.

"We care enough about them to let them do everything they can do for themselves," Mary said.

Asked what she regards as the greatest reward she sees from OPARC's work, Mary said, with little hesitation, "These people learn that they can have value, and that someone cares about them—and it's respectful caring."

The OPARC operation is funded by its own revenue from customers, state monies, United Way funds, and corporate, foundation and individual donations.

State cutbacks have ripped the association's $3 million annual budget. The administrative portion of the budget is an amazingly low 13 percent, and the small staff has not received pay increases in two years.

The Hafif Foundation of Claremont recently offered $10,000 to OPARC if its supporters could raise that same amount on its own. Quietly and quickly, OPARC responded by raising nearly $16,000.

Meanwhile OPARC goes on. It's there for grieving parents as well as their children.

And yes, the healing progress can almost be measured.

As in a hospital, the angels of OPARC provide life. But they also provide what is similarly cherished:

Dignity.

Julie And Other Angels

When I looked into her eyes I was reminded of Chris Evert-Lloyd.

To say she resembles the tennis player would not quite be the whole truth. The prettiness is there, though in a different way.

But those eyes—they could have been staring down the line at Wimbledon. Or smiling—as eyes can do—during a post-match interview in the Paris sun.

As we talked I could see a measure of kindness behind that look. An unmistakable compassion was there, I thought.

Her blonde hair was brushed with a hint of red that was so faint one would have missed the color altogether had the morning sunlight not slanted in just right.

Her shoulders caught the straight hair and spread it out like a silky train.

This young woman is Julie Sampson, 26, and she is full of vibrancy—like a spring garden.

I had not known of her until recently when I read a news account of her entering a scrungy bar and being subjected to a scene of blood, booze and bodies.

A guy lay dying, four others were wounded, and the time was at hand for Julie to do what she does very well—save lives.

Medics routinely grapple with life-giving judgment, medications, and instruments while enveloped in blood, mud and the wet of night.

Or muster all of her considerable skills in the attempt to do so.

Julie, you see, is a paramedic.

She's as steady as she is refreshing—as tough as she is tender.

The bar had been sprayed by bullets fired from the gun of a crazy. No time to think about that now—just keep life in the victim who had been most seriously wounded.

That night Julie was in the midst of her third consecutive shift with the Pomona Division of the Cole-Schaefer Ambulance Service.

Earlier in the evening she had the sorrowful duty to pronounce the death of a mother and her baby who had been struck by a train.

It had been a difficult shift.

The man in the shot-up bar died after Julie and her partner had taken him to the hospital.

My learning of Julie's dreadful work that night stirred my curiosity. What is this young woman like? Why does she do what she does? What is the reality of life out there in what might be defined as deadly human disarray?

I drove to Julie's regular Diamond Bar station early one morning recently where she was ending another 24-hour shift.

She was dressed in a paramedic jump suit—black with reflector stripes at the cuffs of her sleeves and pant legs. The reflectors are there to keep the wearer from being run down on a dark street or highway while struggling to keep death and life apart.

Our visit was a telling one. I learned something of kindness, concern and the heart of a woman.

Julie said she likes her work because "I've always wanted to help people. This is the most direct way I know of doing that."

"In an emergency we often are the patient's first touch with advanced medicine," she said. "We are expected to be fast, comforting and right."

It's not always easy, she said. The medics' skills are not played out in the sterile environment of a full-lighted emergency room.

Medics routinely grapple with life-giving judgment, medications, and instruments while enveloped in blood, mud and the wet of the night.

Sometimes there is no illumination other than what comes from of their own ambulance headlights.

Julie's most rewarding experience results from "field saves"—the act of restoring life to someone whose heart has stopped.

"It's like being on top of the world," she told me, explaining the rush that accompanies the rare experience of giving back life.

Julie is quick to praise fellow paramedics as well as people from other agencies. "Pomona Fire (fighters) are angels," she said, referring to the crews with whom she works 911 calls.

"I always tell the Pomona Fire guys that they're angels."

Somehow I think Julie knows something of angels.

Her eyes told me so.

Mickey

Mickey Gray didn't know his father loved him until after the old man died.

Mickey, in fact, just lived with the idea they hated each other.

His own feeling for his father seemed to be certain. It was a deep hate. And Mickey believed it was very real.

It always had been that way. Mickey thought his father didn't understand him. Never had. When Mickey was young, he wondered why he had been born.

But when his father died, Mickey felt a loss. There was grief, but not a whole lot of it.

After the funeral a family member brought Mickey a small box, and said that his father wanted him to have it after he died.

"Aren't you going to open it?" his brother asked.

Mickey couldn't understand why his father would want to leave him anything at all. He took the box to a private place and removed the lid.

The contents of the box included a lock of Mickey's childhood hair. Old report cards. Notes Mickey had written to his dad. Dates of things that had happened in Mickey's life.

Mickey cried.

He was devastated. "A lot of love was coming out of that little box," Mickey says.

"It wasn't him who hated me," he said. "It was my fault. But it was too late when I found out.

"If I had seen through it all—seen the love, I would have been a very different person."

But no. Mickey was in reform school at the age of 13. Later he spent more than seven years in prisons (including San Quentin) for shooting two people in a Laundromat holdup.

He drank, took drugs, sold drugs, and was always ready to fight.

He traveled through life with a gun in his hand and a knife in his boot. His life was a pile of debris. Trash.

> *She took him in nearly 30 years ago in the way you would take in a junkyard dog that had been run over.*

49

Today Mickey is the pool maintenance man for Upland High School. He is 53, and a whole gulf of years separate him from those dark times.

He is married, has four children and a 14-month-old granddaughter. And he loves them all.

"I am at peace with myself. I'm at peace."

His life was changed by the love of his wife. She took him in nearly 30 years ago in the way you would take in a junkyard dog that had been run over.

Now Mickey tells young students his story of life in human sewage, and how he crawled out of it by learning how to respect himself so he could learn how to be loved by others.

He hopes his story will keep kids out of gangs and out of jail.

I listened to Mickey speak to a sophomore class at Upland High last week. His presentation to the students is rough. The language comes right out of the cellblock shower room. The horror of prison life is not in any way sanitized for the 15-year-olds. There were tears among the kids.

Mickey stands there, a mountain of a guy dressed in a black leather jacket, gray and black T-shirt, jeans and western boots. A tiny earring is backgrounded by a tattoo on Mickey's neck. The Fu Man Chu mustache is thick.

"I just wish someone had talked to me the way I am talking to you now," he told the class.

The students asked some questions when his talk ended. When the bell rang they all applauded.

Mickey's been working with students for the past several years, giving 20 or 30 programs a year. "If I can just save one kid . . ." he said to me as we walked across the campus later.

He has collected more than 3,000 letters from grateful students who have heard his story. An excerpt: "You really had an influence on this class. After hearing all the stories about jail and drugs, I don't think a single soul in this classroom would want to go through all that."

And: "I went home last night and gave my mom and dad a hug, and told them I love them."

Finally: "I respect you deeply."

Mickey sometimes wonders why he thought he didn't love his dad when he was a kid. He thinks maybe the love was there, but he didn't know it.

That was the real tragedy.

And that's why Mickey still keeps the little box.

An Interchange for Mr. Mikesell

Rising high off the flat of the valley between Fontana and Ontario is a mountain of steel and concrete. It is massive and twisted, but somehow orderly, created with great precision and design. It is in a constant state of rumble.

This heaving structure is four levels of freeway interchange. It's where the I-15 and I-10 meet to mix and scramble vehicles before sending them and their occupants north, east, south and west toward tomorrow.

This modern-day intersection is the terminus of I-15's Devore Cutoff that extends from Cajon Pass and skirts San Bernardino on its way west to the I-10.

A jillion cars must pass through that swirl every day carrying each driver to a rendezvous with the next event in their lives.

I traveled by there last weekend, headed toward my own next event. It was a fishing trip with someone with whom I have been acquainted for many years.

Dan Mikesell was a man whose thinking and vision of things were, somehow, out there ahead of the rest of us.

The sun, glinting off auto windshields as we passed the huge interchange, gave it light and motion.

While looking forward to our trip, I recalled that a friend once told me you are never really able to know a man until you have fished with him.

It is true. For by the time I had finished parts of three days of bait and boat with Dan Mikesell I believed I had at last come to really know him.

Many people remember the 83-year-old Ontarian. Across a couple of decades he was a member of the county Board of Supervisors representing Fontana, the foothill communities, as well as residents of Lytle Creek, Mt. Baldy, Upland and Ontario.

He left the board for a time while he made an unsuccessful try for a State Assembly seat.

Then he was elected to the city council seat in Ontario, where he served two years (1960-62) as mayor before returning to his supervisor's chair.

I can recall that Dan Mikesell was a man whose thinking and vision of things were, somehow, out there ahead of the rest of us.

When he was elected to the board in 1954 he realized his district was stirring and stretching from an agrarian slumber.

He saw a different future. He contemplated new and dramatic needs and goals while others remained tethered to the way things had always been.

Dan's thoughts then were of modern transportation, airports, regional parks, and a community that must prepare itself for a great socioeconomic awakening. He and his own drummer marched right on.

Dan saw the advantage of regional political thinking and interdependence. He strode the halls of government in Sacramento, Washington, D.C., and Los Angeles and other cities as well as those in the county seat.

His mark is deep on the Ontario Airport, county complexes located in this valley, the Guasti Regional Park, and yes, he is the virtual father of the I-15 Devore Cutoff.

"I didn't do those things alone, of course," he said as he tied a leader and treble hook to his line. "I guess you can say I was a good pusher and nudger."

His politicking and lobbying took him away from his district much of the time, so an awkward sort of estrangement developed between him and his constituency.

His appetite for fence mending and brute politics was behind him, so he retired from office in 1976.

As we returned from the High Sierra the other day I pondered this history and this man. Too much of his work, I thought, is forgotten or unrecognized.

Sad.

Then we passed the mountain of steel and concrete—the mixer of travelers with its four levels of bustle. I recalled that it has a name. By state legislative action several years ago it was, and is, officially designated the *Daniel D. Mikesell Interchange.*

Federal law prohibits the placement of a roadside sign noting such tribute. I'm told that law may be changed, and such a sign may some day be placed there.

I hope so, because it will mark a deserved and fitting tribute.

Woody

I was surprised the other day when I received a greeting card from Woody.

Woody is a dog.

Because I am accustomed to my mail coming from real people, I didn't, off hand, expect to hear from a cocker spaniel. I assumed (and still do) that Woody was assisted in posting the card by his 7-year-old mistress.

The girl is beautiful, and her soft flax-colored hair looks if it's been kissed by the summer sun. She is the daughter of dear friends of ours, and she and her disarming eyes made off with my heart long ago.

One cannot help but love her. And if you love her, you love Woody, too, because they go together the way biscuits and honey do.

The child's young dog is small and handsome. His golden coat matches the color of his little mistress' hair.

Despite any role the girl may have played in mailing the greeting card, the mark of Woody's paw was on it, which by my reckoning, established the greeting's authenticity.

"This one's from Woody," I said matter-of-factly to my wife as I went through a stack of cards. She didn't look up from her morning newspaper.

Woody and I share a matchless relationship. We nurture an understanding that just sort of hangs there between us undefined and unrecognized by anyone but him and me.

I think Woody likes me because my gift to him is genuine compassion, care and patience. The reason I like him is infinitely clear—he's so dumb he needs all the consideration and clemency one can assemble.

It may seem cruel to describe Woody in that manner, but I say it with all the kindness I know. You see, Woody does things like sitting still on the lawn while the sprinklers soak him to the skin.

"He thinks it's raining," his mistress told me. And said the girl's father: "It's just that he doesn't seem to care."

Me? I simply dry Woody off afterward while he tries to lick my face.

Many months ago the mistress' father was trying to call Woody to him from where the dog sat in a puddle of water on the sidewalk. "C'mere, Woody. C'mon, boy!"

Woody just sat there in the water, head cocked to one side as if he were listening to a phonograph.

Woody just sat there in the water, head cocked to one side as if he were listening to a phonograph.

"Try sic 'em," I suggested.

"Sic 'em, Woody!" the man said as the slapped his knee with an open hand. Woody ran right over.

"Attaboy, Woody," I said as I gently petted him. "Good boy."

Woody looked up at me and smiled.

"Where does Woody sleep?" I once asked his little mistress.

"He sleeps in different places every night," she said.

"How come? Most dogs sleep in the same spot all the time."

"He can't remember where he spent last night." she said.

"Don't pick on him so much," the girl's father once chided me. "He's just a pup."

"But he's been a pup for three years now. He'd better hurry up and improve or he's going to become permanently dumb," I warned.

Woody and his family once spent a Sunday visiting his mistress' grandparents. I was there, and the men among us tried to play bocce ball, which is a lawn game that's sort of a cross between shuffleboard and bowling on the green.

We were thwarted in our attempt to play, however, because Woody kept sitting on the game's jack ball.

He didn't put it in his mouth and run off with it as a normal dog would do—he just sat on it.

Later in the day he ran into a small retaining wall while chasing a butterfly and knocked himself out. He wasn't seriously hurt, and we got in a game of bocce ball before he came around.

When we left the party I called "sic 'em" to Woody so I could tell him good-bye. He came to me, smiled and licked my hand.

I've always known Woody is lovable. And now I know he's very kind as well.

Otherwise why would he have sent me that card?

A.T.

Mister Richardson's given name was Almon. But few people ever called him that.

Many never knew what his first name was, and I suppose there were some people who didn't even know he had one at all.

He was simply known by his initials, "A.T."

And there was a legion of young colleagues who never considered calling him anything but "Mr. Richardson."

But I think if such a moniker had existed in A.T.'s time, he would have been known as "Mr. Pomona."

For nearly 70 years A.T. Richardson's hand was on the city's newspaper, the *Progress Bulletin*, or its predecessors.

> *I remember him best as being an infinitely kind man. There was no minus about him.*

As it turned out, A.T.'s hand during that time was also on the city as it journeyed through tough times and good—from not much more than rows of vines and groves to a pumping economic center and a community of good life.

He went to work at the old *Pomona Progress* as a beat reporter at the age of 23. That was in 1903. It was the year the Wright boys flew the world's first airplane and President Teddy Roosevelt signed a treaty that led the way to the construction of the Panama Canal by the United States.

A.T. had just finished his studies at Pomona College where he worked his way through school as a sometimes gardener and by waiting tables at the college dining hall.

For the next 69 years A.T. worked for, or owned the newspaper. He was in his office at the *Progress Bulletin* building on Thomas Street the day before he died in 1972. He was 92.

The mark of his work is still on the city. And it will endure. He served on governing bodies for the library, hospital, junior college and chamber of commerce, and was quietly active in other community endeavors of high purpose.

The weight of his influence and the power of his newspaper formed sort of a personal apparatus that brought a lot of good things to a lot of good people.

He was modestly proud. But in light of all that made him well-known,

I remember him best as being an infinitely kind man. There was no minus about him.

An old friend of his said to me the other day, "If you were in a room crowded with people and A.T. entered, you suddenly could feel his presence there. The whole place seemed to be lifted up."

There were those who revered him, but being a newspaperman, he also was capable of attracting wrath. Once an unhappy politician threatened to toss A.T. out of his second-story office window.

He was inherently generous and fair. During the Great Depression he found himself unable to meet the newspaper's payroll. So he paid his employees with IOUs —IOUs that business people around town told A.T. they would honor.

A.T. then accepted the IOUs in return as payment for advertising. The arrangement worked well until the company lawyer told A.T. he was, in effect, printing his own money and the practice was illegal.

Nonetheless, no one went hungry during a particularly bad time.

Earlier this month a noble group of newspaper publishers gathered at the Four Seasons Clift Hotel in San Francisco to honor A.T. They elected him to the California Newspaper Hall of Fame.

A.T.'s name now resides with good company, such as William Randolph Hearst, Edward W. Scripps, Joseph Knowland, James S. Copley and a few others.

But also wandering the wings of the hall is Crombie Allen, an early-day publisher of *The Daily Report* in Ontario. Both the *Progress Bulletin* and *The Daily Report* are forerunners of the *Inland Valley Daily Bulletin*.

The elevation of A.T. to such honor is a surprise to no one in the newspaper business. It was, they knew, inevitable that he would be inducted sooner or later.

But to hundreds of those around the valley who knew and loved A.T. best, it somehow seemed that he had been in his own kind of hall of fame for some time.

Santa Claus

I discovered a place the other day where down in the dumps doesn't have a chance. You can't be blue there. If you're unhappy when you arrive, it won't last. If your mood is bad, get set for a change.

It's the people. There are only a handful of them, but they radiate a certain goodness. Their hearts are light. They put a smile on their world.

If you're grouchy, cheer up or get out of the way. If you don't want to smile, don't go there.

If is a tidy stone building on the east side of Ontario. Its interior looks sort of like a shed or small warehouse.

It's a workshop. Tools are everywhere. Paint, fabric, parts and pieces are scattered about in controlled confusion, and the people who work with the disarray produce mild wonder.

"Our salaries aren't much, but our bonuses are big."

The folks there do their jobs with determined efficiency, pausing only from time to time to let their high spirits run through the rooms like a flight of sparrows looking for a place to land.

About seven or eight of them are regulars, but others sometimes join to help out.

It would be bad manners to report here that the people are elderly. So I won't. But I would guess you could find some Vaughn Monroe music in their record collections.

The more-or-less boss of the work crew is Bob Fritz. He's 80. Some of the others are younger. I wish my heart were as young. While I was there, the group's collective sense of humor was at work on the subject of their ages.

What this crew does, day in and day out, year around, is very simple. They repair, refurbish, rebuild and renew a mountain of toys, bikes and dolls to be given away to thousands of kids each Christmas—kids who otherwise might not have much of a Christmas.

Helping Bob are Joan Hale, dolls; Marjorie Ball, games; Frank Jones, wheel toys; Kelly Hartwell, bonus toys; Jim Van Dusen; bicycles, and Bill Kelber, assistant to the bike and wheel guys.

There have been a million words written of this group—Santa Claus, Inc. And that is not too many.

When you read "incorporated" you might envision a hefty agency with staff, offices, vehicles and payroll. Consider these facts:

—There is no executive director of Santa Claus, Inc.

—There is no staff, no payroll.

—There is only one telephone.

—There is one loaned pickup that is used to collect donated repairable toys.

—Although hundreds of people donate toys to Santa Claus; its nucleus is less than 20 steady volunteers.

—Nearly 5,000 children received gifts from the organization last December.

—The entire operation is funded by donations from individuals, service clubs and businesses.

The gifts are distributed each Christmas in neighborhoods that are within the boundaries of Chaffey Joint Union High School District.

Families who receive the gifts must qualify and must apply. During a four-day period before Christmas, parents from qualifying families come to the Santa Building at 1330 E. D Street, and select the gifts. The children need not know the origin of their Christmas presents.

Santa Claus, Inc. is 36 years old, and has brought its brand of happiness to tens of thousands of youngsters.

It began in the 1950s when local elementary school students collected canned goods each holiday season for distribution among families that needed them.

Someone thought it might be a good idea to include a doll or two with the canned food. That first year there were 13 dolls distributed.

Last December Santa Claus, Inc. distributed 1,200 dolls.

The joyful workers in that East D Street building never see the children they help.

"Our salaries aren't much," said one of the unpaid Santa's helpers, "but our bonuses are big."

Claremont's Quiet Place

I have always regarded the botanic garden in Claremont as something of an on old friend.

It has been a comfort when trouble intruded, a place to let joy soak in during better times, and an environment where one can submit to life as it is and be grateful for it.

Of course the garden is much more than serenity.

For one thing its real name is Rancho Santa Ana Botanic Garden, and its director (Thomas S. Alias), scientists, staff, gardeners and an assemblage of volunteers are dedicated to the garden's essential purpose —furthering research, education and conservation.

I once thought the garden was one of Claremont's cherished secrets' simply because by some standards it is a low profile institution—no billboards, no commercials, no grand entrance nor bands or balloons. Not much toot to it.

No commercials, no grand entrance nor bands or balloons. Not much toot to it.

Items in the garden's gift shop run more to books and paintings than they do to T-shirts and coffee mugs.

People could drive by the place a hundred times (1500 N. College Avenue) and never know they have passed it.

The garden's 86 acres is a wonder of nature and hard work by human hands.

It's trails, ponds, conifers and grand oaks provide a mass of knowledge as well as comfort.

But don't look for manicured lawn and riotous bedding plants here. It is no Butchart Gardens nor Augusta National Golf Course.

The beauty here is an abundance of California vegetation the way Mother Nature meant it to be.

I went there one Saturday morning in an attempt to bring some order out of a week that had become unraveled. There was a mist in the air, but no rain, and the garden was particularly quiet.

It was cool but not cold. I walked down the Riparian Trail and later came to settle on a bench overlooking a gully.

The bench is in a favorite spot of mine on the Woodland Loop. From there the view permits the eye to wander away from the garden, move among native flora, trees and chaparral, then rise to the ridges of the San Gabriels.

Moments later I was on a small cliff looking down to a level below where conifers steeple themselves into the sky.

The regal Majestic Oak also is there, and it spread out as magnificently as a banyan tree in Hilo. A marriage ceremony was unfolding under the tree's gnarled branches and heavy foliage that protected the small group from the mist.

The only sound I heard was a murmur—obviously the celebrant's voice. My presence was not noticed. As I looked down on that peaceful assembly, I felt my unraveled week settle back into place.

I moved on before the kiss.

When the garden is not being kind to romantics, it is a lively place of study and conservation.

About 100,000 people visit the place each year. Admission is free. In excess of 10,000 take advantage of guided tours and a variety of seminars, study groups and symposia that are conducted throughout the year.

The next heralded event is a Southern California wildflower show scheduled April 18 and 19.

The collection of these native flowers will represent the diversity of wildflower species from the coast to the desert, according to Rebecca Caughman, who recently welcomed me to her office at the garden.

The exhibition will be the largest show of its kind in the southern part of the state, Rebecca said. The show is new this year.

The land on which the gardens flourish is partly (about half) owned by the Claremont Colleges and partly by the garden itself.

The institute is supported largely by grants and research contracts. Chief horticulturist at the garden is Bart O'Brien, and the scientists with whom he works serve on the faculty at the Claremont Graduate School.

Rebecca, who grew up and still lives in Claremont, told me she has a love affair with the garden just as I do.

She recalls visiting there as a child and later as a student.

She was married in the garden not long ago—over by the rustic home center. Near a stream and a small bridge.

It's a good place to start.

Don Drysdale

Super Dodger fan Mark Williams called me Saturday to tell me Don Drysdale was gone.

Vin Scully, he said, made the announcement at the top of the eighth inning of the Montreal game.

Mark, I thought, was seeking solace. So we talked. Just talked.

During our somber conversation, Mark remembered that there are not many Brooklyn Dodgers who are still in Los Angeles. The count, we decided, is sentimentally small now. Drysdale had been among that number.

"It's just about down to Vinny, Sandy Koufax and Tommy Lasorda," he said.

After Mark hung up, I thought about Brooklyn's move to L.A. in 1958 and what it meant to all of Southern California, including us out here in the valley.

His windup and delivery looked to me like a threshing machine at work in the Kansas wheat.

It was when we drove all the way to the Coliseum to watch the Dodgers play on a football field. A blooper to the 25-yard line was good for a base hit, and one of Wally Moon's pop-ups over the high, left field screen was a certain home run.

It was when Chavez Ravine was still a place to live, and when Gil Hodges always blew a kiss to his wife as he crossed home plate near the goal line after hitting a home run.

It was when Jim Gilliam was still called Junior, and when guys, especially guys like Don Drysdale, played baseball with their hearts.

It was a time when Duke Snider, Johnny Podres, Drysdale, Koufax and other bums moved across the country to see if the Screwball Belt was ready for big league ball.

It was a time for cold beer, salad and garlic bread at the Trojan Barrel before the game—or for wine and cheese on the lawn at Exposition Park outside the stadium.

But as much as anything it was Drysdale's time. He won 12 games that first year in Los Angeles, but four years later he won 25.

In 1961 he was paid $32,000—more than any other pitcher. He thought more of his team than he did of money, but in 1966 he and Koufax held out for $100,000. And in those days "holding out" was something like nuns striking against the pope.

To my untrained eye, I always saw Drysdale as an immense man, and his windup and delivery looked to me like a threshing machine at work in the Kansas wheat.

He certainly wasn't a gangly pitcher, but I thought he moved like a giraffe falling downstairs as he came off the mound. It took a lot of twist to put the big body in motion.

He didn't throw pitches, he launched them.

His long right arm cocked back in such a fashion, young batters couldn't tell where the pitch was coming from until it was too late. The ball usually was past the plate before the batter could say, "darn!"

Drysdale was 6-foot-6, and he thought the batter's box belonged to him first, the batter second.

He hit a lot of guys, and some say he did it on purpose. He once was described as a "Headhunter with a Horsehide."

"Drysdale never hit anybody unintentionally," a guy once said.

Some say he was mean. I think "fierce" is a better word. He just thought losing was something for the other guy to do.

He could field the ball while lying on his back in front of the mound, and sometimes in late innings with guys on and two out and another pitcher in the game, Walter Alston would send Drysdale in to hit a home run.

Friends say there were two Don Drysdales—the aggressive athlete on the field and the gentle, like-to-laugh companion off the field.

His later broadcast interviews showed his passion for the game and the men who play it. Once he pitched more than 58 innings without allowing a run, and 20 years later when a young Orel Hershiser broke that record Drysdale passed the mantle with dignity and grace.

He pitched for the Dodgers for 14 years. Then in 1969 his arm went sore and was finally used up.

Like Drysdale himself, his heart came in twos—he had one for the body and one that throbbed for the game.

The one for his body failed him the other day.

But the other one never did give out.

The Beach

I learned recently that I was to experience a couple of days of unexpected and temporary bachelorhood.

Volunteer work was to take my wife out of town for the weekend and she unselfishly suggested I plan something special for myself while she was away. She's that kind of pal.

I first thought I might take in a matinee—see a cowboy show, eat popcorn and drink a soda. The last time I did that, Bill Boyd was the star, and the movie house served Nehi at the lobby snack bar.

But, turning to grander possibilities, I scrubbed the matinee idea and called my neighbor and ol' buddy, Schumway, to see what he was up to that weekend.

I learned that he, too, could fashion a furlough from the rigors of Saturday's call to chore. We decided on a trip to the beach in a camper.

"Don't knock it—914 bottle tops and you've got a pound of aluminum."

We didn't mind the rain.

Schumway and I have been known to get into mischief together. Nothing serious or naughty. Just things like blowing up wieners in the microwave. Or dropping the metal oars over the side while we were in the middle of the lake.

Things like that.

With tools we are hopeless. Once we tried to repair an old pickup of his. We ruined it, and he had to sell it for scrap.

One Christmas Eve we accidentally locked ourselves in his garage while we were assembling a bicycle. There was nothing in there but Schumway, me, the bike and the fridge where he kept his Colorado Kool-Aid.

It was a cold night. We didn't get out of there until that nice Mrs. Schumway came home from a family visit around midnight.

When we finished with the bike, we discovered we had the pedals on the wrong sprocket. "It'd take Superman to ride this sucker," Schumway said.

As we pulled away from the curb on our beach trip, my wife called out, "Are you sure you two will be safe?"

"What did she mean by that?" Schumway asked.

"Who knows?"

By the time we arrived at San Clemente the rain had stopped, and sun glinted off the sea. The sky was patched with blue and white.

Schumway got out his Geiger counter and headed for the beach.

"What are you looking for, Uranium?"

"This a metal detector."

"What do you find with it?"

"I look for coins, rings, watches and other stuff people have dropped in the sand. You know, expensive things."

"What do you find most?"

"Bottle tops."

"It's going to take a long time for that thing to pay for itself," I said.

"Don't knock it—914 bottle tops and you've got a pound of aluminum."

"C'mon, Schumway."

After finding 13 pop tops and some chicken wire, we decided to abandon the hunt and assemble the new bike rack for the camper.

It's difficult to believe, but we managed to put the rack together upside down. The bikes fell off when put 'em up there. Just fell off.

We did the work again, making greater reference to the picture on the box the rack came in. At last we got it right.

As we tidied up after the job, Schumway said, "What are these little things that are left over?"

"Rivets."

"Lordy, I hate to have things left over. Makes you think you left something out."

"With our luck, they probably hold the whole thing together."

"I wonder how many of these it would take to make a pound," he said.

"Just gimme the rivets, Schumway."

"How'd it go?" my wife asked when we returned.

"Great. We had a nighttime fire in the fire ring and sang *Someone's in the Kitchen With Dinah*, and *Li'l Liza Jane*."

"Not at the same time, I hope."

"As a matter of fact we did—ol' Schumway doesn't know the words to *Li'l Liza* and so we . . ."

Before I could finish, I noticed my wife had left the room.

Centro Basco

I made the attempt to challenge Thomas Wolfe's admonition the other day by trying, in a certain way, to go home again.

In great part, I think the effort worked.

It was on the downside of an afternoon, and I had just completed a meandering excursion through some of our valley's farmland.

I wanted to reaffirm that those fields were still there, unchanged, peaceful and serving as a reminder that we are all, in one manner or another, tethered to the earth.

The trip was reassuring. Between those tranquil farms and the busier part of the valley north of there lies the old Centro Basco Hotel in Chino.

It sits there squatted on the south side of town, and it was part of my route home that day.

The handball games have also withered and been pulled down into time.

I wondered if the hotel, which also was a bar and restaurant, is still a daily settling place for Basque sheepherders.

Do they still play *hogoi eta hameka* (31) in there? I asked myself. And do they drink wine, sometimes from *botas?*

I stopped to see.

The front portion of the building is much as I remember it when I was a younger man, and frequently visited the place.

A certain amount of frolic and good times was a constant guarantee in those days.

Basque food was served family-style at long tables in dining rooms adjacent to the bar.

I was comforted to learn that the practice survives.

Located toward the rear of the building today is another and more conventional dining room.

It is more polite than the front portion where the bar and long tables are more earnest and tied to the past.

In earlier times, the young sheepherders would draw curtain to their day and play handball on the courts in back of the hotel.

Those contests would be followed by games of 31 in the bar, some drinking and perhaps a friendly fight. Really.

Then the evening meal would follow at the long tables.

Several people were at the bar when I walked in the other day.

They were mostly old men.

Only a bit of English was being spoken, which lifted the prospect of my finding a piece of the past.

The bar was quiet, the old men pondering whatever was in their minds.

Pierre Berterrectche, Centro Basco's proprietor, was tending bar.

Pierre is a 73-year-old Basque who served in the French Army during World War II.

His eyes are moist—not from sadness so much as from pure time.

Speaking through a straight and seemingly perpetual grin, he talked of his sheep herding days in Wyoming where he settled 45 years ago.

He moved to the Chino Valley in 1955.

"Are there any Basque sheepherders left here?" I asked.

"They are mostly gone," he said sadly, but for some reason the smile did not abandon him.

"The young ones got married, moved away—went home," Pierre said.

"Why?" I asked.

"No sheep anymore—just houses where they were."

The handball games have also withered and been pulled down into time.

The Basques who were in the bar during my visit were not sheepherders. They were not young.

They showed no interest in a friendly fight. Nor handball.

They were not, in fact, speaking Basque when I entered the bar. It was mostly Spanish or English.

But when I showed interest in their days gone by, they shifted into the Basque language with ease, and, it seemed to me, with well drawn pride.

Someone thought to get out the 31 jug containing its assortment of little numbered peas, and the little cup began to flash quickly around the bar.

The game was played with increasing flourish now.

A lively vitality struck the place and a certain amount of frolic stirred in the room.

A lot of laughter.

My new friends shared some history of their language and Spanish/French homeland with me.

And they laughed. And the 31 cup banged against the bar as the old men shouted with particular glee.

When it was time for me to leave, some of the old men turned to say good-bye —"*Ikus artio! Ikus artio!*"

Outside, as I walked to my car I could hear the increasing boisterousness in the background.

And I wondered if song would soon follow.

Tell A Child

> *Ohno Natsuko strained to hear as Upland Mayor Robert Nolan explained the inner workings of American city government. "I just want to be able to speak English," said the shy exchange student.*
> —From a *Daily Bulletin* news story.

Standing on the slopes of the San Gabriels or in their broken canyons a hiker can sometimes hear a faint rush among the manzanita.

The rustle seems incongruous because there really is no sense of wind. It is as if the shrubs are whispering among themselves.

Such sound reminds me of a garden wind chime that provides light music even in apparent stillness.

I have come to know this eerie state of things from time spent walking among the mountains north of the valley. This strange sound without wind can be a quiet prophecy of fury on the way—a storm in full gale that will rip and rend as it thunders from the east.

How anyone can work up a hate for such a person as Ohno Natsuko is beyond understanding.

Now there may be another sort of warning hanging over the land. It has come in an anti-Japanese temperament among a limited fragment of Americans a strange sound without wind.

It was a whisper at the start of things, but could it be rising toward an ugly roar? Is the wind kicking up? Is certain fury on its way?

It is unimaginable that we Americans are beginning to hate again as we did in the past while moving through the darkest tunnels of our history.

Yet Lt. Gov. Leo McCarthy has defined hate crimes in California as "epidemic," and the *Daily Bulletin* newsroom continues to receive an increasing amount of sinister mail and anonymous telephone calls directed at a variety of minority groups in the Inland Valley.

The home of a Japanese-American family in Claremont has been desecrated. Other signs of miserable activity have been recorded and investigated in our midst.

As frightening as anything, perhaps, is the relatively accepted practice of Japanese bashing in public, and from Americans in high places.

The anti-Japanese prejudices have extended to other Asians, and an increase of intolerance of people of a variety of racial origins is prowling our valley.

How anyone can work up a hate for such a person as Ohno Natsuko is beyond understanding.

To lack compassion for all fellow Americans with Asian beginnings is more unthinkable. But the lacking is there.

Jay Kim, the mayor of Diamond Bar, is an American, but his longest roots end in South Korea. Kim is seeking a seat in the United States Congress, and he acknowledges the issue of race will figure in that contest.

While discussing the subject last week, Jay said this to a journalist: "The majority of American people do not support this kind of craziness."

"I'm just as willing to die for this country as anyone. All I ask is that they accept me as truly American."

And why not? That's what he is.

There is no justification nor ground for genuine, malignant hatred, including being a victim of the recession, being without a job, Pearl Harbor or any other discomfort, nastiness or even horror wrought by unwanted circumstances of another time.

By accepted definition, we all are aligned with one minority or another. So if you accept justification, excuse or acquittal for certain hatred, then you should be prepared to hate everyone at one time or another.

A hideous prospect.

Accepting the premise that wiliness to practice inhumanity must be taught or learned, it would then follow that intolerance must be unlearned.

Or even better, not taught in the first place.

Let us beware of the warning of the breeze.

Tell a friend.

No, tell a child.

Pigeon's Roost, AKA Pomona

Joe Firman, who was a friend and colleague of mine, wasn't an official historian, but he was a good thief.

He knew where and from whom to steal history, and he did it with considerable talent and glee.

Joe died a few years ago, but not before he wrote a zillion columns for the *Progress Bulletin* in Pomona. He called his work "Rattles and Straws," which defined the column's personality of profound potpourri.

Although the subject of his column varied, he sometimes wandered the crevices and caves of our valley's past, and in so doing he made effective use of the memories of local residents who knew it best.

Stealing their knowledge and passing it along to readers was Joe's gift to the rest of us.

Now it is time for me to steal from my old friend himself.

Indian Hill Boulevard in Pomona was once called Alexander Avenue.

Through the help of old-timers Bill and Betty Southworth, who ARE official historians, I found myself reading a piece Joe wrote years ago about some history that is forever entwined with the names of streets and places around the valley.

For instance, Pomona once was known by some of its neighbors as Monkey Town and, later, Pigeon's Roost.

But it was first called Rancho San Jose when it was part of an 1837 Spanish land grant.

How, then, did Pomona finally come to be called Pomona?

Joe wrote that when the village officially became a town, a contest was conducted to name the place. He reported that one Solomon Gates, a local nurseryman who was fascinated by mythology, won the contest by suggesting the town be called Pomona after the Roman goddess of fruit.

Before Pomona was incorporated, large tracts in the area were acquired by the Los Angeles Immigration and Land Cooperative Association. That was in 1875.

If you wonder where some of the streets in Pomona got their names, look no further than to the list of the people who were officers of the land company: T. A. Garey, president; L.M. Holt, secretary; and directors J.E. McCombs, J.F. Gordon, George C. Gibbs, R.M. Towne and C.E. White.

Louis Phillips was an owner of a considerable amount of land, and he left his name not only on Phillips Ranch, but on Phillips Boulevard.

When Joe's Rattles and Straws column recorded this history, little did he realize that the ranch would someday become a virtual city.

Ganesha is another Pomona name that is readily recognized. A high school is named for it, and so are a park and a street. The origins of that name can be traced to P. C. Tonner, who gave the city three acres of land for a park in 1890.

The town citizenry was so pleased with the gift they asked ol' P.C. to give the park its name. Wrote Joe Firman: "An authority on classic lore, Tonner chose Ganesha, after Ganesh, the Hindu god of water and good things, as well as a remover of obstacles."

Now who's going to argue with Joe Firman?

Some names of streets and thoroughfares have been changed over the years, and for some reasons the changes were sometimes upsetting to old-timers. Holt Boulevard in Ontario, for instance, was known for decades as A Street.

"I'll call it A Street until I die," an old-timer told me the other day.

Joe noted that the San Bernardino Freeway was called the Ramona Freeway when it was completed in 1957. "Traditionalists, romantics, and historically minded people protested in vain," Joe wrote in his column.

And Indian Hill Boulevard in Pomona was once called Alexander Avenue, but was changed to Indian Hill because that is the street Alexander joined in Claremont.

And why Indian Hill in the first place? The street traverses a small rise of land north of what is now downtown Claremont where the area's last Indian village stood.

All this came to me with the help of my friends, the Southworths, who live in Ganesha Hills.

It's a nice place, and they are a nice couple from whom to steal a bit of history.

Joe would have been proud.

Death In The Texas Sand

Garth Brooks has restored honor to my name. But in the process he has taken from me a certain measure of joy.

No longer must I sneak listening to country music. I can do it right out in the open.

I am, in a sense, out of the closet.

Super singer Brooks has made the listening of his kind of music an OK thing to do. He and his style have legitimized country. That's what I read, anyway.

Legions of normal people accept it now.

Because of Brooks and some other innovators, I no longer must look in both directions and into the rear seat before I turn on the car radio and settle back for a little Willie Nelson, or George Strait, or K.T. Oslin on my way to work.

When his wife started the car, Hank Williams Jr. and his rowdy friends blasted her clear into the back seat.

But it seemed more fun to sneak the music. There was a certain excitement about it. It sounded better like that—the way olives taste special when they're swiped off the table before anyone has been seated for Thanksgiving dinner.

I have enjoyed country music for so long that I can remember when I thought Porter Waggoner was good.

For many years I have shared my yen for country with my neighbor, Schumway. But like my wife, that nice Mrs. Schumway would not permit country and western to be played in the house.

Schumway and I both would have to go the tool shed or the garage if we wanted to tap our toes to a George Jones tune.

Every time I spotted ol' Schumway coming home with his hat pulled down, his collar turned up and wearing dark glasses, I knew he had been out shopping for a Waylon Jennings tape, or maybe it was Merle Haggard.

He played the tape in the family's second car, which was mostly reserved for his use. Every radio push button in his car but one was set to a country music station. A single button was reserved for classical music.

When he arrived home he routinely would shut down his C-and-W music and push the classical button. That was just in case Mrs. Schumway had to use the car.

Once he forgot to make the switch, and when his wife started the car, Hank Williams Jr. and his rowdy friends blasted her clear into the back seat.

Ol' Schumway had to do the dishes that night.

Sometimes on Saturday mornings he and I would go to Flo's at the Chino Airport for breakfast. Just for the biscuits and gravy and other down-home food, we told our wives. The real reason, of course, was to get in a bonus session of country during the drive down there.

Those were the days you didn't want anyone to know you were drawn to country songs.

I mean, can you imagine explaining to your mother-in-law why you like such lyrics as *It Ain't Easy Being Easy?*

Or *All My Exes Live In Texas, That's Why I Hang My Hat In Tennessee.*

Schumway particularly enjoyed *It Ain't Love, But It Ain't Bad.*

Another favorite: *You Are Smooth As Tennessee Whiskey/ You Are Sweet As Strawberry Wine/ You Are Warm As A Glass of Brandy/ That's Why I Stay Stoned On Your Love All The Time.*

My sons are mostly rock fans, and my wife leans toward such normalcy as Vivaldi and Brahms.

In earlier days that situation left me with the mark of being sort of a low-brow musical loner.

My 10-year-old dog, who doesn't like rock, enjoyed driving around with me on weekends, both of us listening to the likes of *You Walked Across My Heart Like It Was Texas.*

But now all that has changed. I found out not long ago that even our priest is drawn to western song.

He has been for a long time, but like me, he harbored his musical preference in secrecy, fearful to let the truth out.

Now he and I sometimes drive along listening to Garth Brooks sing *It's Boots And Chaps And Cowboy Hats . . . They Call The Thing Rodeo.*

But somehow it was more fun sitting in the wheelbarrow there in the tool shed and listening to Marty Robbins sing about death in the sand outside Rosa's Cantina in El Paso.

All by myself.

Ima's Trophy

When Ima Davis of Claremont died last summer her passing was noted by an 18-line obituary.

She was 93.

Dick Liles, also of Claremont, was troubled and saddened by the brief account of a life that moved through nearly a century.

Dick's frustration worked away at him until he decided to write me a letter about Ima. He wasn't angry, he said, just sad.

"An obituary only about 18 lines long makes people think you didn't amount to much," he wrote, "but she did."

"Her death probably means nothing to most people, but it did to me."

The beginning of Dick's and Ima's friendship is rooted in the 1940s. World War II's last rattle had gone into history, and the world was tired.

Ima's sons were athletes at Bonita, and her pride in them was immense.

Dick, about 12 at the time, delivered the Pomona *Progress Bulletin* to subscribers in his own west Claremont neighborhood. He rode his bicycle along the route—rain or shine.

He called on his customers individually to collect his earnings. "It was in those days I learned how hard it was to make a buck," he told me the other day.

"The first $100 I ever saved came from that route, and it took me the better part of a year to do it."

Ima and her husband, who was a downtown businessman in Claremont, were among Dick's newspaper customers. Their home was about a block away from Dick's house on 10th Street.

In that time, the village was so small that just about everyone in town knew everyone else who lived there.

Dick's dad, Everett, owned and operated Everett's Shoe Repair in the village for 46 years. The shop was something of a hangout for folks in town, including Ima's young sons, who sometimes acted as baby-sitters for Dick and his brother.

"Every time I went to her house she would give me cookies or candy and milk," Dick said.

"What a wonderful mother she was—just like mine was."

Much has changed since that time. The children are grown.

Dick's older brother, Bob, recently retired from Pomona First Federal, and Dick works for Laird Construction Co. in Rancho Cucamonga. He still lives in Claremont. And now Ima is gone, and her children have moved away.

Dick remembers attending junior high school when it was housed in the same building as Claremont High.

The high school and junior high were where Griswold's Claremont Center now stands at Foothill Boulevard and Indian Hill.

Ima's sons decided to forego classes at Claremont High and, instead, enrolled at Bonita High School in La Verne.

"Those boys rode their bikes all the way up to Bonita every day," Dick said.

Bonita, incidentally, later moved, and Damien High took over the building. Damien is still there.

Ima's sons were athletes at Bonita, and her pride in them was immense. She was proud of the boys' sister, Mary, too, but Mary was not as interested in athletics as her brothers were.

Later, when Ima's sons went away to college, is when Dick called regularly at her home.

"She would take me through the house," Dick told me, "and show me the room the boys shared.

"There were medals all over the walls."

"There was no sport these twin brothers were not great in."

But Dick recalls one special treasure that meant something very special to him. Ima displayed it proudly in a special place in her living room.

It was the Heisman Trophy, which, of course, is the highest honor that can be bestowed on a college football player.

Her son had won it in 1945.

He played for Army.

His name is Glenn Davis.

An Angel In The Night

The clock and calendar of my life have prevailed sufficient time for me to become a bore if I did not take great care to avoid it.

I have used up enough years to have grandchildren. I have served in the military, traveled some, and even para-kited across the bay at Acapulco.

All of these minor adventures are the stuff of which boring conversation is made. Who really gives a hang? Nobody.

Now comes the epitome of such matters. I have had The Operation. And accounts of surgery are certain bore-makers.

I would not refer to that unhappy event here, but some reader inquiries have made me feel obliged to account for the absence of my commentary in this space for the past couple of weeks.

My life was never in real danger during my illness, but a routine malady went awry enough to require some swift and skillful work with a scalpel.

I am assured I will survive and regain full and perfect health.

Some events during my hospital sojourn might be noteworthy. Such as the visit from my neighbor and ol' buddy, Schumway, whose idea of cheering me up was to say, "Better to laid up than laid out."

"Thanks, Schumway."

Or when I was upgraded from wearing an open-back gown to real pajamas with tops and bottoms. The outfit was so large that the huge pantlegs piled up on my feet, and the leggings had to be rolled up four or five times before they cleared my ankles.

The shirt hung somewhere below the kneecaps and almost reached the rolls of the pantlegs.

When my sympathetic wife saw me in that goofy outfit she simply said,

"One size fits all, I see."

Ol' Schumway said, "If you'd just put your hat on backwards someone would probably call you cool."

"C'mon, Schum, help me find my cane."

I turned and walked away from her. I didn't want to talk to her, fearing she would become mortal, and I didn't want that.

And then there was the angel. She came to my room each night. It was always late, and the lights were dim and the halls were quiet.

I was alone each time she visited, which caused me to wonder if I was the only one who ever saw her, or if she was indeed real.

She was utterly thin and gowned in a habit of some sort. It was white with the exception of a splash of black at the top. She was old, and her thin, long face was made pure by the prettiest smile I have ever seen.

She seemed to float, not walk. And her skirt sort of glowed in the dim light. She had the accent of a Dublin cop, but her words were so soft and slow they might have been carried along on a spring breeze from Glocca Morra. She didn't preach. She didn't pray. She didn't offer me a tract of any kind. Just: "Ere ye betta t'dey, ere ye?"

When I assured her that I was, she softly said, "Aye, thenks be t' Gawd." Then came that radiant smile and she was gone.

One late night I left my room for a painful but mandatory walk, and I noticed the angel standing alone some distance from me in the hallway. No one was in the hallway but the two of us.

Her back was to me. She was just standing there. Silent and alone.

I turned and walked away from her. I didn't want to talk to her, fearing she would become mortal, and I didn't want that.

Nonetheless, curiosity overcame me and I turned to ask her name. But she was gone like an apparition. The hallway was empty.

I never saw her again.

Later in the night as I lay in my bed listening to the quiet ping of the IV pump, I thought of that smile, and of the soft voice.

I own them both forever now, I thought.

Then I closed my eyes and began to measure the abundance of my good fortune.

Fred

The kitten was so small when he came to live with Fred that he looked like a little puff of white smoke as he curled up at his master's feet.

That's why Fred named him Smoky.

It was 18 years ago. Now Smoky's gone—his life came to an end last summer.

And Fred cried.

"That was a tough one," he said.

Smoky and Fred lived together for 17 years. There was a bond between them, and it just sort of hung there in an undefinable state of affection.

The lives of Fred and Smoky came together in New York City, and in 1979 they moved west and settled in Upland.

His exuberant salutes and his stocky body's never-ending motion send motorists along with an unmatched flair.

Now all that remains is the memory of Smoky and the license plate on Fred's car that reads: "Smoky O."

The "O" is for Orellano," Fred's last name.

Fred will be 70 in December but he is not old. The youthful state of his big heart and his eyes that smile just before the rest of him does keep him younger than most.

When he isn't smiling he's laughing.

There are others who share his 30-year bachelorhood—a golden cat and an old Pomeranian, both of whom Fred dearly loves.

Still, Smoky was special.

Fred's children and their children live in nearby cities. But mostly his world is the little house in Upland. He farms a small vegetable garden in his back yard.

The tomatoes, zucchini and peppers are planted in earth-filled wooden boxes sitting atop stone blocks.

"Why didn't you just plant your garden in the ground?" I asked him the other day as he showed off the tomatoes' yellow blossoms that promised the bounty to come.

"Its the gophers. If I planted my garden in the ground I'd have gophers like this," he said spreading his hands in the air as if he were holding an invisible watermelon.

Then he laughed, his eyes squinting almost shut but looking out from his salt-and-pepper beard that matched the color of his thick hair.

One probably would not suspect that Fred commands a certain amount of fame. He is known and loved by thousands. He is a school crossing guard and sees to children's safety at Seventh Street and San Antonio Avenue.

But his other deeds outdistance his duties by a million miles.

He is a guide, a friend, an entertainer, an inspiration and blur of activity as he preside at that corner. His arm-waving greetings, his exuberant salutes and his stocky body's never-ending motion send motorists along with an unmatched flair.

He would remind you of the old greeter at Laguna Beach.

And every driver responds to Fred—it's a honk, a wave, or a politely offered hail and then the motorists are swiftly gone.

They'll be back tomorrow.

The children, too, are greeted, and they return the salutation.

"I love kids," Fred said, "and they keep me busy, young and healthy."

He said they mostly call him Fred, but some call him Smoky because of the license plate.

"I like that," he says.

Fred is soon to begin his fifth year at the corner, and he never has seen a child hurt there.

"I'd let a car hit me first rather than one of my kids," he said.

A retired liquor/deli manager in New York and California, Fred says he loves people because he's always dealt with them in a close way.

And the love is returned. The walls leading to the bedrooms in his home are decorated with scores of cards from children. Gifts, handmade and purchased, sit on every shelf in his living room.

Inside the front door in the entry hall hangs a huge greeting card given to him at a school luncheon held in his honor last year.

The card is signed by 600 students and simply reads, "We Love Fred."

Before I left, he said, "You know, it doesn't cost anything to be nice."

That's right, I thought, and as I drove away I figured out that if Fred were paid for his kindness he would be rich beyond his wildest dreams.

Actually, I think he is already.

The Village On The Hill

A trip to the Padua Hills Theater and Restaurant is something like visiting a friend in the hospital—there's life there, but it is not as full, pulsating and animated as one would hope.

The place is, as one might say, not its old self.

I drove up there in the morning sun the other day to walk the theater's halls, empty shops, studios and grounds, all shaded by a forest of ancient olive trees.

Had the old spot on the hill lost its charm, I wondered?

I found much of the charm is hanging on, but age is at work. There is unsettling evidence of decay on some of the outbuildings.

As I walked through the famous pergola, I felt the silence of the grounds much like I felt the warmth of the June morning. There was a certain vacuum there. The quiet was heavy.

All these happy, swirling events brought vibrancy to Padua Hills since its founding in 1930.

How many thousands of those in our valley are unaware of Padua Hills' existence, I thought. It's only a short drive —north on Padua Avenue off Base Line in Claremont.

Thousands—some historians put the number at millions —have strolled those grounds, dined there, married there, applauded the Mexican Players and been entertained by artisans from glass blowers to strummers of mandolins.

All these happy, swirling events brought vibrancy to Padua Hills since its founding in 1930.

The Mexican Players, perhaps best known for their annual Christmas production of *Las Posadas*, performed regularly until the 1970s.

Theater events finally played out, and now the grounds and halls are used sporadically as a picturesque site for weddings, receptions and parties.

Richard and Cheryl Lindholm still use the kitchen for their catering business—Chantrelle's, as well as host the on-site weddings and receptions.

The site offers a rustic setting for happy private gatherings.

The looks of the settlement have sometimes been compared to a small Mexican village, yet it seems to have a Spanish mission feel about it.

Its beginnings can be traced to the purchase of 2,000 acres of brush land in 1929 by a group of 20 Claremont residents who wanted to protect the area from unwanted development (sound familiar?).

The theater was part of the preserve and was founded to provide a place for community theatrical productions. A restaurant, shops and studios were added.

Ginger Elliott, executive director of Claremont Heritage, told me that in 1935 the nor profit Padua Institute was formed to promote friendship and mutual understanding between Mexico and the United States.

With that action the Mexican Players came into existence. They were all young men and women of Mexican descent from throughout Southern California. Some were from Mexico.

In the earliest days, the performers served guests in the restaurant as well as appeared in their famous productions.

Now all of that is gone.

Ownership of the open space as well as the theater and its grounds has fallen to a partnership of which Pomona College is a part. The partnership has agreed to sell Padua Hills and 1,300 acres to the city of Claremont.

The plan now, according to Sharon Wood, Claremont's director of community development, is for the city to purchase the acreage, sell 125 acres of it to a developer of fin homes, then keep the remainder as open space. "We need to sell the 125 acres," Sharon said, "so we can afford to purchase the rest of the site."

What will become of the theater and restaurant? No one knows at this time, but it will be rejuvenated and preserved for some type of community use—perhaps a conference center, Sharon said.

Whatever its future, the little village on the hill surely will keep its charm.

It is just too good to be lost.

She's Still A Lady

She's tired, and there are some wrinkles, but she's still a lady.

She's sort of like the day after the party. The glow is faintly there, but the signs of rough times show through like a stain on the carpet.

You look at her the way you do your old college sweater. It was a knockout once. Now it doesn't look so good.

She reminds me of a gracious matriarch of the theater whose star has slowed down, dim and pulsating now. The bright, steady glow is gone.

When you think about her, the past is infinitely better to contemplate than the present.

The sounds of her high times and gaiety, parties and pleasant winter days in the sun are faded now, like the music of a marching band that has passed by and now is a couple of blocks down the street.

The best is over. Age has done its work, leaving behind what's left of an era that once was golden.

I'm talking about the Ontario National Golf Course, which came through the early '60s the way Scarlet came down the stairs at Tara.

At the pinnacle of those good years the place was known as Whispering Lakes Ontario Public Golf Course. Governors dined there. Celebrities teed up there. The best entertainers performed at the club's Royal Tahitian, and superstar golfers knocked their drives a hundred miles.

Gary Player competed there. So did Johnny Miller, Champagne Tony Lema, Bob Goalby, Doug Sanders and some of the really old guys like George Bayer and Gardner Dickinson—even Lloyd Magrum.

In 1962 Al Geiberger won the Ontario Open, an official PGA event in those days. He was 25 then.

Player was in the tournament, and he was only 27.

Years later Geiberger became the first (and only the second) golfer in history to shoot a 59 in competition.

Player is now one of four golfers in history to win all four major tournaments. Both Player and Geiberger still play the over-50 senior circuit.

Gregg Norman was only 12 months old when Geiberger won at Ontario.

Ontario National Golf Course came through the 60s the way Scarlet came down the stairs at Tara.

Whispering Lakes was home to the Royal Tahitian, a club that attracted entertainers such as Ray Charles, Duke Ellington, the Righteous Brothers, Sonny and Cher and Louis Armstrong. And many others.

The Royal Tahitian often sold out. Luaus, held beneath palms between the putting green and the 10th tee, were so popular that clubs, employee groups, private parties and other organizations signed up weeks in advance in order to obtain accommodations. It was difficult to rent the dining room for class reunions.

The course was, and still is, a test of good golf. The greens are small and trapped more than many courses in the valley, and there are a couple of lakes to avoid.

In a way, the course is prettier than it ever has been, with its weeping willows and cypress trees now grown and standing as a stately signature to the course.

And that is why I believe she is still a lady.

But technically speaking, the fairways have fallen to decay, and weeds and other elements have scarred the layout.

The putts don't roll as true as they did when the stars played there.

The city of Ontario owns the land where the golf course is located (Riverside Drive west of Archibald), but the entire place is leased to Ontario National Golf Course.

The lease will expire at the end of this year, and the city will soon decide the fate of the one-time jewel.

The City Council last month talked of an assortment of possibilities. Among them was the transformation of the golf club into a full country club offering not only golf, but tennis, swimming, racquetball and first-class restaurants.

Can a golden era be resurrected? Will the lady make a comeback?

Let's hope.

Phillips Mansion

About three miles beyond the edge of the little town in which I spent my childhood sat a one-room schoolhouse. It squatted there on the road to Deer Creek and was, appropriately enough, called the Three-Mile Schoolhouse.

Our town was so small that everyone knew everyone else, and that familiarity extended to families who lived on outlying farms. So I knew most of the kids who received solid instruction in basic skills at the Three-Mile Schoolhouse.

They were sons and daughters of poor farmers, and they attended class wearing coveralls and high-top shoes, or no shoes at all.

A couple of the kids rode their ponies to school.

The historical society, like knights on steeds intervened and rescued the house from dozer blades.

As I recall, there were about 12 or 15 children in the school. They attended grades one through eight. Miss Bailey was the only teacher, and for some reason, her students seemed brighter than those of us who attended the Union Grammar School in town.

The Three-Mile students came to town with their parents in rickety cars on Saturdays to buy groceries and supplies, and the next day they would come to town again to attend Sunday School.

That's when the rest of us would see them, and hope they would invite us out to their places some weekend so we could play in the hay and swim in Cattail Creek.

Golden days of delight.

I whistled through that town not long ago. An interstate now skirts the community leaving it undisturbed and abandoned seemingly to rest in another time.

The interstate rumbles within a few hundred yards of where the Three-Mile Schoolhouse stood, and now a fast food market and gas station sit where the little white school building had been. The school, the ponies, the kids and Miss Bailey are all gone now. It seems they were there a zillion years ago.

Asphalt and neon have taken their place

Miss Bailey's instruction in phonetics is no longer available there, but you can buy a six-pack and a tank of unleaded real quick.

I have heard that once, long after my family had left the town, there was a move to save, preserve and restore the little school, but the voices of those who advocated the preservation of that small piece of history died out like whispers.

Now the town wishes it had the Three-Mile Schoolhouse back. An old story.

This brings us, by my circuitous route, to the three-story Phillips Mansion in Pomona.

Beth Page, president of the Pomona Valley Historical Society, and others are petitioning the City Council to help save the old place.

The once elegant home, built by the Phillips family in 1875, sits on what was once the southern environs of the original Rancho San Jose that flourished when this valley was part of Mexico.

The mansion is located at 2640 Pomona Boulevard, between Temple and the Corona Expressway.

The Phillips family bought what was left of the Rancho in 1866 for $30,000, and lived in the spread's original hacienda until the mansion was built. It was the first brick building in what we now call the Inland Valley.

During World War II the home was converted to apartments, and in the 1960s the site was rezoned for industrial use and the house was scheduled for destruction. The historical society, like knights on steeds, intervened and rescued the house from dozer blades.

But now the mansion is falling to ruin. Beth Page and her supporters have planned a $500,000 restoration project, and are asking the city for $40,000, plus contacts to apply for more financial help.

There is an unalterable fact about bits of tangible history: once the school, the home, the old post office, or whatever, is gone, it is gone forever.

Let's hope that 50 years from now people in Pomona won't have to wish they had the Phillips Mansion back, the way people in my little home town wish there was still a Three-Mile Schoolhouse.

Winter On The Mountain

Cowboys, according to Willie Nelson, carry a fondness for clear mountain mornings.

Bless 'em. I share the love.

What comfort it is to be part of a dawn in cool woods, their silence disturbed only by breakfast sizzle or the occasional signals of jays and other forest tenants announcing they're ready for the day.

Most of us who live in the valley are closer to crisp forests, shadowed canyons, lively creeks and mountain mornings than we realize.

Mt. Baldy Village, slung in San Antonio Canyon like a giant eagle's nest, is only 11.4 miles from the Madonna statue at Foothill Boulevard and Euclid Avenue in Upland.

Just 16 miles separate the statue and the Mt. Baldy ski lift 8,000 feet above the level of the sea.

I thought I might have heard faint music and laughter, like the sound of a music box from another room.

I know the distance, because I laid measure to it the other day during an early morning drive to the clouds where winter was still on the mountain.

The trip was made in a morning mist that soon separated me from the valley and a disordered, sometimes zany world.

I rose to clean air and quiet.

Two cars overtook me just north of the tunnels, and they were soon gone in the mist that was thickening to fog. It was as if the vehicles had passed out of existence. Phtt!

Now there was no traffic. The stillness crept inside my car.

As I passed Mt. Baldy School and approached the first houses in the village, it seemed sleep was on the whole settlement.

Obviously there was some stirring inside the cabins and mountain homes—some here-and-there chimney smoke told me so.

I traveled past the lodges, the bridges, the trout pond, then slowed at the old Chapman Ranch, whose perimeter is traced by a zig-zagging split-rail fence. The ranch never seems to change.

A windmill stands nearby, and along with the entire wooded ranch it brought thoughts of a movie scene.

Are you in there, Ben Cartwright?

Then on to the Ice House Canyon turnoff and the short distance to the ruin of the burned-out Ice House Canyon Lodge. All that remains of it is its native stone foundation and nine front steps that ascend to nowhere.

The laughter and song that often brought pulse to that once merry inn are forever gone.

I stood there on the steps in the canyon's silence, and recalled the many times I enjoyed the lodge. And I thought I might have heard faint music and laughter, like the sound of a music box from another room.

Leaving there, I challenged the route to the ski lift. It's twisty along those switchbacks, and the road raised me to traces of old snow and a forest wet with winter's weight.

Then past Glacier Picnic Area, Snow Crest Inn, Manker Flats Campground to the parking lot at the ski lift.

A few skiers were taking flight to the notch and the ski runs beyond.

The lift was visible only as far as the fourth tower, then the chairs' occupants were enveloped in clouds and taken to their day of fun.

After a few deep breaths of air that had turned cold, I descended to the valley, leaving the mountain morning behind.

The next day I visited Dr. Harvey Good at his biology lab at University of La Verne. Harvey has lived in Mt. Baldy Village for nearly 26 years, and he and his wife have raised their three children there.

Harvey said about 1,000 people live in the canyon. Nearly 80 students are enrolled in the school there.

Harvey and I talked of canyons, old trails, landmarks, campsites, and the backpacking that took us to those places in years past.

When I asked Harvey what is his main purpose for living at Mt. Baldy, he quietly and simply said, "It's the environment. I just like it up there."

The drive from his mountain home to his classroom takes 25 minutes.

"I've made that trip thousands of times," he said, "and I always see something different along the way."

When Harvey said that, I recalled my drive the previous day. I thought of winter on the mountain.

And its purity.

Nice Pills

The youngest house guest we ever entertained for more than a night or two was five years old at the time.

Her sojourn extended over several days during which her mother and father awarded themselves a temporary time away from parenthood.

The child's presence increased the population of our house by 50 percent. My wife and I had been more or less left to ourselves since our sons said good-bye and we embraced a quiet life.

We took it in like a deep breath when the young men departed. That was a decade or so ago.

And now, with our little guest on the way, the number of occupants of our home would again total three.

> *She and I, and an assortment of natural wonders, all came together with a special sort of harmony.*

It can be said with little risk of contradiction, that during recent years the routine of our lives had settled into something considerably stable. We had become, what they used to say, "set in our ways."

The girl's visit required us to apply some adjustment. For instance, our guest's definition of evening activity did not include the McNeil/Lehrer News Hour. Or the reading of Ivan Doig. But we managed.

We looked for Waldo instead. And read of Peter Rabbit and other adventurers.

We also acknowledged to one another that the girl, whose father is our son, was exceptionally well behaved during her stay with us.

She can be, as other 5-year-old girls, tumultuous at times when tumultuousness is not particularly a favored part of the adult agenda.

At her own home she sometimes can behave as Little Audrey does when Little Audrey is bad. But during her visit to our home our guest was particularly civil.

She was, in fact, moving in on being angelic.

We marveled at her demeanor, especially considering the fact she was 250 miles from her Central Coast home.

One afternoon during her stay with us, she and I were sitting in a red wagon under our backyard peach tree.

The autumn sun warmed us as she and I, and an assortment of natural wonders, all came together with a special sort of harmony.

She wanted to know why hummers around my feeder could fly without going anywhere, and I was struggling with the answer. Seeking to extricate myself from scientific explanation of the flight of humming birds, I said to her, "I think I know why you are being so good this week."

"Why?"

"It's those 'Nice Pills' we've been giving you," I said referring to the oversized M&M's we had purchased for her as treats for the week.

"You're just saying that. There's no such thing as Nice Pills. They're just great big M&M's."

"Well, Ken Dean at the drugstore said they're Nice Pills. And he should know. If you take some each day you become real nice, just as you are now."

"Really?"

So the remedy was administered with regularity throughout the remainder of her stay. And it worked.

When the visit ended and the child's parents came to retrieve their daughter, she was displeased. She did not want to leave the sublimity of our house, and the attention she received there.

She was crying.

"Here," I said, handing her some Nice Pills to help her through the unhappy parting, "have some of these now and take the rest home with you."

Quickly, almost miraculously, she quieted down.

Several days later as I was talking to her on the telephone, I asked how her life was going around her house.

"Not so good," she said.

"What's the matter?"

"I'm in trouble with my mom."

"Why?"

"Because I've been bad, that's why," she said with remarkable candor.

"Well, take some of those Nice Pills I gave you, they'll straighten you right out."

Then there was a silence. Then a pause. Then came this quiet, but absolute, deliberate and very serious statement:

"They don't work up here."

Lindbergh In Our Valley

My friend T. Willard Hunter, the author from Claremont, has contacted me regarding his considerable devotion to the subject of Charles Lindbergh.

Willard told me he was interested in my recent mention in this space of Lindbergh's famous flight across the Atlantic in May 1927.

Willard, who has written a book, *The Spirit of Charles Lindbergh: Another Dimension* to be published in April, wrote this to me the other day:

"Lindbergh noted on page 509 of *The Spirit of St. Louis* that he flew via Pomona from Los Angeles to San Diego on September 21, 1927. It was part of his 48-state welcome home tour.

"The way I heard it, W.K. Kellogg (head of the breakfast food empire and operator of the Kellogg horse ranch near Pomona) notified Lindbergh that he had painted big identification letters on his landing strip at the ranch.

"Lindbergh had announced he would try to reach all strips that did this, because he wanted to promote the practice so other pilots would know where these strips were by reading signs painted on roofs and so on.

"Apparently, he did not have time to land at the Kellogg ranch, but did pass over and dip his wings in salute."

Willard suggested a check of our own newspaper files might shed some light on the subject. According to a story I found on Page 2 of the September 21, 1927, edition of *The Daily Report*, Lindbergh did, indeed, stop at the ranch.

Under the headline "Lindy Flys over Fair Grounds and Thrills Throngs," is this story:

"Charles A. Lindbergh, the winged ambassador and his mono plane, the *Spirit of St. Louis*, headed toward San Diego today where a few short months ago the famous flier began his journey on the road to fame.

"Zooming high into the rays of California sunshine at 11:31 a.m., the silver bird became a gleaming streak as it headed southward. Lindbergh landed at the W. K. Kellogg ranch near Pomona shortly after noon. After brief formalities the young ace headed the *Spirit of St. Louis* south again at 12:30 after circling above the Los Angeles County Fairgrounds."

Lindbergh apparently visited the ranch a day after he was welcomed in

> *He did not have time to land at the Kellogg ranch, but did pass over and dip his wings in salute.*

Los Angeles where 200,000 people gathered at Vail Field to see him land.

Another crowd of 500,000 watched him in a parade down Broadway.

But I found a second news story in the September 28 edition of *The Daily Report*, however, that read as if the aviator did not actually touch down at the ranch. The story:

"When Lindbergh circled the W.K. Kellogg ranch near Pomona yesterday, he clinched a verbal contract with the cereal king to give to that community one of the finest airports in Southern California.

"Kellogg had informed Lindbergh that if he would fly low over the Kellogg Ranch that several acres would be given over to the community for use as an airport.

"Kellogg promised further to equip the field with hangars, repair shops and everything else needed.

"Lindy fulfilled his part of the contract," the news story ended.

This later story makes no mention of a landing at the ranch. The earlier story notes an exact time of touchdown, however, giving evidence a Pomona area landing was actually made.

A bit of a mystery. But I trust Willard Hunter a lot.

The later story did indicate, however, that the high-flying negotiations between Kellogg and Lindbergh resulted in the collapse of a plan by a group of four cities and a college to establish an airport on the Union Rock Co. site near Claremont. The communities cooperating in that endeavor were Pomona, Claremont, Ontario, Upland and Pomona College.

When Kellogg promised to build an airport on his ranch, Pomona and Claremont announced their inclination to drop their airport partnership with the college, Ontario and Upland. The cities' airport idea died.

A permanent airport never was built at the Kellogg ranch, but nearly 30 years later a pretty fine college was established there—Cal Poly University.

A Day In The Sun

Thirty-seven years ago this week the San Bernardino Mountains could no longer hold back the dawn.

Then the sun broke the earth's rim and began to work away at the haze that hung over the valley. It was July 4, and forecasters said it was going to be a cool Wednesday.

The early morning haze burned off, yet the thermometer did not reach 80 that day. The temperature dipped below 60 the night before. It had been downright chilly.

Marlene Mariene McDonald had a difficult time enjoying a good night's sleep. She was excited about the events of the coming day when, as Miss California, she would reign as Queen of Ontario's All States Picnic and Parade.

Ontario's mayor, Col. Pete Petersen, was perched atop a convertible. He waved the way the pope does.

A police officer spotted a woman setting up her picnic space at the picnic's New York table at 5:30 a.m. It was cold and barely light, but she had claimed a good spot for her family to watch the parade and enjoy lunch.

The morning was as quiet as that whole era was. In those days Ontario's population was 39,432 (it's more than 140,000 now), and many citrus groves were still being farmed south of Foothill Boulevard.

Some even extended below the brand new San Bernardino Freeway into Ontario and beyond.

There was only one high school in town, and student discipline there was of minor concern.

There was no campus dress code because one wasn't needed. And there were no drive-by shootings because nobody had guns with which to shoot.

Nor did anyone want them. Elvis had just recorded *Heartbreak Hotel*, and a spot on the *Ed Sullivan Show* that year turned the Tennessee truck driver into "The King."

Bill Clinton was 9 years old. George Bush was 32. The Korean War was over, and good ol' Ike was president.

There was not much real war in the world, which seemed to be enjoying a bit of slumber.

The biggest national news that July 4 morning was the discovery that two airliners that had crashed into Grand Canyon the previous Saturday had indeed collided in aloft.

As July 4 warmed, early arrivals began showing up at the site of the All States Picnic, whose table stretched three miles along Euclid Avenue between B and Sixth Streets.

By midmorning the gathering could be described as a crowd. Before the day ended with a dance in front of Gardiner W. Spring Auditorium, 110,000 people had enjoyed the festivities.

Entertainer Leo Carrillo rode as the parade's grand marshal, and the winning queen's float carried Shirley Swank, Miss Missouri. The Ohio queen's float, which had won first place for four consecutive years, placed second and was ridden by Ohio Queen Roberta Neville.

And of course Marlene Mariene McDonald was there, rested and performing her queenly duties.

Ontario's mayor, Col. Pete Petersen, was perched atop a convertible. He waved the way the pope does.

The event drew national attention, and picnickers arrived from as far away as Tennessee and Vermont. There was an abundance of visiting as people passed among tables that represented every state in the union, Canada and Mexico.

The annual picnic and parade will be held again Monday, and organizers expect a crowd of not much more than 15,000.

Some old-timers believe picnic crowds were larger in the 1950s because there was less competition for family entertainment then.

Disneyland did not open until 1955, the Dodgers were still in Brooklyn, the Angels played minor league ball, Magic Mountain was still a mountain, and the Quakes were yet to become real people.

Besides that, the All States Picnic and Parade was free. It still is. And it's still great. I might drop by there tomorrow and look for yesterday. But yesterday won't be there. Neither will Leo Carrillo nor Col. Pete.

But I might find some folks at the Missouri table who know something of my ancestors.

Remember The Guns

The sifting of the ash and aftermath at the Branch Davidian compound will be a task that consumes more than several days.

Or weeks. Or even months.

The nation will agonize through that exercise for years. It will be a task of such enormity that it may never really come to a comfortable conclusion.

Measuring the complexity of what happened at the compound, and what led to death in the Texas sun, will bring law and religion to deliberate test.

Citizens' rights, moral virtue and the depth of the human mind, dignity and conscience will also be subjected to a special kind of public scrutiny.

In the beginning, the investigation will be a terrible hunt for what once were people. Then the probe will turn to a pursuit of truth during the unfolding of horrid events.

There were guns in there that could conceivably shoot down aircraft. David figured he was ready for war. Bring on Goliath.

And that search will wind through tunnels of great twist, some of which travel in and out of our own community where sect leader David Koresh not long ago resided in La Verne with some of his religious followers.

In the backwash of Monday's horrible end of things there will be investigations, and there may be arrests, trials and convictions.

Congress will conduct hearings. Law enforcement agencies and their practices, judgment and action will be questioned. People on lofty perches of government position will be called upon to explain themselves and their performance in the storm of calamity.

It will be an acute time of viewing with alarm. And I hope, that among all this fuss, someone remembers the guns.

During the past few days we have read little about Prophet Koresh's collection of heavy arms.

But earlier newspaper reports told us he had gunnery that could shoot missiles through walls. Within the compound were a couple of single-shot 50-caliber rifles that could blow a man away at a mile and a half.

There were guns in there that could conceivably shoot down aircraft. David figured he was ready for war. Bring on Goliath.

If the Davidians had been prevented from buying and storing the weapons in the compound, there would have been no reason to send agents there to get them in the first place.

The moral, political and reasonable assumption here is that David Koresh should not have had all that weaponry. And an equally fair assumption is that if he had not been that well armed, we would not be counting all those burned corpses in Davidianville.

If there are laws that would have kept certain kinds of weapons out of Koresh's little fort, then those laws are not tough enough.

The right of Americans to own guns is well enough defined by the U.S. Constitution—at least well enough that no U.S. Supreme Court has ever said otherwise.

But there is nothing in the Constitution that says the right to own weapons includes the right to abuse their use.

It is legal, after all, to mount public protests in this country, but it's not OK to burn down an abortion clinic.

The use of alcohol is not illegal, but abusing alcohol can result in a jail sentence.

Speech is free, but don't impair that right with malicious lies and accusations.

Where does the right to own guns end and the right to operate combat weapons and make private war begin?

Is it logical to argue that it's OK to operate weapons of war? If such logic is accepted and extended, then it will continue to be OK for just anyone to collect arsenals and use them in the preservation of any cause they wish to embrace. Even anarchy?

Perhaps a sense of maturity, a process of learning can come from the ashes of Texas.

Perhaps a new priority is out there somewhere.

Perhaps we can learn that individual rights can sometimes go wrong. Bad wrong.

A Stillness On The Land

The whole world woke up to a different kind of thunder 49 years ago this morning.

The sound of war seemed to rattle the whole universe as the largest military assault of all time lumbered and stumbled into massive conflict on France's western shore.

The beaches of Normandy were about to be battered into stark immortality.

It was D-Day, June 6, 1944. Nearly 180,000 soldiers, who called themselves GIs, dogfaces, ground pounders and sailors and flyboys, crossed the English Channel from Britain in rough seas and angry skies on a crusade to rescue Europe from World War II.

Those men, brave and young, hoped to find the end of misery somewhere out there in that uncertain mist and on that dangerous and frightful road to Berlin.

There were no structured worship services that morning. Most of the people just came and sat there.

About 4,000 ships and 11,000 airplanes participated in the invasion, which has come to be known as the Longest Day.

By the end of June a million allied troops had reached France and were holding on. But not much more than that.

Today you will read about the landing. You may see a movie that attempts to re-create the unbelievable eruption of bombs and bullets on those tortured beaches.

Or you may view a TV documentary devoted to that memorable and frightening time.

You certainly will be immersed in the invasion's history a year from today—D-Day's 50th anniversary.

But what sometimes is left out of all the remembering is what D-Day was like at home. While beaches called Utah, Omaha, Gold, Juno and Sword rocked and belched in fire and chaos, America was held by a strange quiet.

There was a stillness on the land. No bands played to bolster hearts or to summon a synthetic kind of courage.

No cheers rose for the boys at Normandy. Just that stillness.

The landing took place while most people of what we now call the Inland Valley slept. It was Tuesday morning when they awoke to the news.

The valley night had been cool, but 90-degree heat was forecast for later in the day. The sky was clear.

Then the doors began to open at churches. Their parking lots began to fill with cars, and even bicycles.

There was no particular coordination of the somber assembly. People just came.

From the tiny San Secondo D'Asti Catholic Church in Guasti to the largest churches of Pomona, the doors simply opened and people went in.

At 5 a.m. the bells began to ring at the Temple Baptist Church in Ontario. After a while they stopped so visitors could keep their own kind of silence.

There were no structured worship services that morning. Most of the people just came and sat there.

The hush was not limited to our valley. The whole nation was quiet.

President Franklin D. Roosevelt wrote a prayer. He gave it to his friends of the press at the White House and asked them to tell the country that he would read the prayer that night on the radio.

The president asked all Americans to read along with him while he recited the prayer.

California Gov. Earl Warren described the events on Normandy's beaches as "the most solemn hour in the history of our country."

Editors at the *Progress Bulletin* in Pomona and *The Daily Report* in Ontario posted late war bulletins in the lobbies of their newspapers.

There was, of course, no television at the time.

The Daily Report published an Extra during the night, a rare event for a newspaper that small.

The edition greeted most readers when they awoke to the news Tuesday morning. There was just a single advertisement in the newspaper's four-page Extra, and it was purchased by Fallis' Department Store on Euclid Avenue in Ontario.

The text of the quarter page ad was simple and brief "God bless our boys and grant early success to the enterprise they have this day so bravely begun."

The "boys" were mostly kids then. Now they're in their 70s.

That is except for the ones who never came home at all.

Lois

When news came Wednesday that Lois Snider had lost her long fight with cancer and she will be buried Tuesday, I discovered I could not recall any other time she had lost a battle.

She may not have always won, but in her magnificent way she never was defeated.

In anything.

To Lois, defeat was something to be rejected out of hand, and worked into something good. Perhaps she has not really lost this latest struggle. Victory is in it somewhere, and she will find it.

I knew Lois from a time when we were both young. I was sent to interview Lois' mother, who was, believe it or not, a wing walker.

Just four us were there in Lois' home—Lois, her mother, Emily; Lois' sister, Mary Boyd, and me.

The down times she has known have helped her arrange life's priorities into a magnificent alignment.

It was a tidy house on the west side of Ontario, a city in which Lois later was to serve as mayor's wife and first lady for 12 years.

When the interview concluded and I left Lois' home, I remember thinking I had just met three of the most remarkable women I've ever known.

I still think that.

A few months ago I experienced a chance meeting with Lois, her husband, Howard, and Mary. Later I wrote something of that meeting, and looking over those words this week I felt they are as appropriate now as they were when they were first set down. Here they are:

Within the personality of Lois Snider is her incredible ability to attach unquestioned virtue to any and everything in which she believes And that simply means she is a extraordinary saleslady with great heart.

If I were to undertake a venture that required sales, Lois' talent would be the first I would enlist.

She could sell matches to a gasoline tank inspector—boxing gloves to a harpist. She wouldn't, but she could.

She certainly could sell support for her husband's political career.

She also could, and did, win help and endorsement for a multitude of noble causes.

Her optimism is legendary. As her sister said the other day, "Lois has two 'nevers' —she never wants anyone to hurt, and she never wants to hear 'no.' "

Lois just won't give up.

Our political swords crossed sometimes, but they never cut into our friendship.

It is not known by everyone, but Lois has dealt with unhappy times the same way she has dealt with all other of her challenges. And she has had more than her share of unhappy times.

She can sift something good from every circumstance, even if it is just a reaffirmation that her friends are still her friends.

According to Lois, adversity—her own as well as others—is something to face down and somehow to be taken apart until some strength can be drawn from it.

The down times she has known, including the loss of a young son, have helped her arrange life's priorities into a magnificent alignment.

She has always been able to do that. It's a gift.

Now Lois is in trouble. She is ill. Very ill, and today or tomorrow she will return home from one of her regular stays at the City of Hope where she takes not-so-fun-at-all treatments.

Last week, the day before she was to enter the hospital, I found her, her husband and her sister, Mary, at lunch. It was sort of a last good meal before the doctors put the hammer down.

We talked of some of the fun parts of our lives. And she was optimistic as ever.
She looked for a laugh and found one. We all did. There she was, grabbing adversity by the throat once more. Her heart was as great as ever.

The encounter was sentimental.

As I left, I thought almost aloud: *They say she is ill, but I think she is the wellest person I know.*

The Doctor

When I was 6 years old I had my tonsils removed while I lay on an ironing board in the kitchen of our home out in the country.

A mask of ether brought me merciful sleep during the surgery, but the post-operative misery balanced out the comfort of my slumber.

I still remember.

The whole experience was the epitome of an early-day version of out-patient surgery. Way out.

I thought of this adventure the other day as I listened to Ron Sackett, president of San Antonio Community Hospital, deliver a speech on the nation's crisis involving health care costs.

Where I spent my childhood there was no health care crisis because there wasn't much health care to buy.

And if there was, people just paid for it when they could.

Occasionally a farmer slaughtered a hog, and we'd all wind up at grandmother's house eating roast pork.

The little town produced its own brand of single-class society—everyone was poor. Hard times were so universal there was nothing in town to covet, which eased a considerable amount of stress, tension and social competition.

We all just sort of managed together somehow, and enjoyed a now hard-to-understand kind of contentment.

There were only two doctors in town—my grandfather and his brother-in-law (it was the latter who removed my tonsils).

There was no real hospital. If either of the two doctors were required to perform surgery much more complicated than an in-the-kitchen tonsillectomy, they would cart their patients off to a hospital 60 miles away.

The patients would be transported by an ambulance owned and operated by the town undertaker.

I can remember that about the only difference between his ambulance and his hearse was the color. One vehicle was black, the other was a lighter color.

Babies in that town were born in their mothers' bedrooms, and the ladies next door always seemed to be there to help my grandfather with the delivery.

Toward the end of his life, my grandfather, who was my mother's father, could boast he delivered nearly everyone in town. He was everyone's friend.

He also claimed a successful practice of predicting the sex of unborn children. He never told anyone how he did it, but once he said to me privately, "Remember, you're half right for starters."

Near the edge of town was an old, two-story house with many rooms. It was called a hospital, but it really was not much more than a place for folks who needed a lot of bed rest and a nurse.

It probably had six or eight beds in it. And it was white. The little hospital was a place where some people in town went to die.

People paid my grandfather and my great-uncle when they could, but that wasn't often. It was not uncommon for a farmer to call at my grandmother's house offering freshly killed geese or other wild game.

The meat was, of course, payment for my grandfather's services, but that was never mentioned. My grandmother would simply say, "Thank you so much," and she would tell her husband about the visit later.

My grandfather may have saved the life of the man's child at one time. Few of us ever knew.

Some of the food donated by farmers found its way down to my own parents' table, so we all were pretty well fed on geese, pheasant, dove and sometimes even venison.

Occasionally a farmer slaughtered a hog, and we'd all wind up at grandmother's house eating roast pork.

Many years later while passing through that little town, I stopped at my grandfather's house. I found him in a coma. "I went to call him for dinner," my grandmother told me, "and he just wouldn't wake up."

It had just happened.

I called the undertaker, and we took my grandfather out to the little hospital at the edge of town.

We took him there in the light colored vehicle, and we placed him in a clean and comfortable bed.

He died in his sleep there three days later—just before Christmas. He was 82.

I believe he was one of the kindest men I have ever known.

Birding

Upland's singular celebrity, Hank Childs, gave me a copy of the latest edition of his book the other day. And with his autograph on the title page he encouraged me with these words: "Start birding Now!"

Some people believe real men don't eat quiche. Others think real men don't watch birds. Well, I don't know if Hank eats quiche, but he watches birds. And he's a real man.

He is known as the Bird Man of Upland, a mantle laid upon him several years ago by *L.A. Times* writer Jack Smith, with whom Hank has jousted for several years on the subject of bird sightings.

In 1972 Smith spoke at Chaffey College where Hank was a vice president. Hank introduced the writer, who sometime during the day said he had once spotted a grackle near his Mt. Vernon home.

Couldn't be, Hank told Smith. The limits of that bird's western migration is the Colorado River. A friendly and extended argument ensued and, as it turned out, Hank was right.

"Congratulations, you now have a life list of one. Welcome to birding!"

Writer Smith ultimately capitulated and wrote a column about Hank, himself and the grackle he had never seen.

The two men have been friends ever since.

Some time later Smith devoted a chapter to Hank in one of his books.

One of the chapters in that book describes the Bird Man's feeling about the legendary account of the swallows returning to Capistrano on St. Joseph's Day each year.

"They return any time they damn well please," is Hank's view of things.

Hank Childs is a professional bird watcher, or "birder," as devotees of that hobby and pastime now prefer to call themselves.

The credentials Hank carries could fill a small bird book. He spent 14 years at Chaffey College before his semi-retirement in 1983.

Hank is now a professor emeritus of Chaffey, and lives with his wife, Helen, a birder in her own right.

Helen calls her husband Henry.

The Bird Man of Upland has written dozens of papers and texts on the study of birds. And his latest book, *Where Birders Go in Southern*

California, is in its second printing. It can be purchased at the Book Worm in Upland or borrowed at the library.

It's a must for birders.

The 230-page volume categorizes what species of birds can be found where and when.

Saturday morning Hank and an array of local birders will spend the day participating in what is called the Christmas Count.

The Count is a national (and beyond) event in which birders record sightings in assigned areas. It is kind of an annual bird census, and the results are published by the National Audubon Society in its periodical, *American Birds*.

The way I understand it, bird watching is not like, "Gee, look there at that sapsucker. Aren't his wings pretty?"

As Hank said, "It's more like collecting sightings the way some people collect stamps or baseball cards. It doesn't have the monetary value, but it's great fun."

It's similar to hunting, but nothing is killed.

To serious birders, their "life lists" means everything. A life list is nothing more than a record of all species of birds the watcher has recorded in his or her lifetime.

I told Hank my wife and I had seen some odd-looking small birds in our yard a couple of weeks ago, and I described them to him. "Those were bush tits," he said. "Congratulations, you now have a life list of one.

"Welcome to birding!"

That evening I told my wife I might take up bird watching. "Really," she said without looking up from her book. Then I explained how the life list works, and I told her my list was up to one—the bush tit.

"How large is Mr. Childs' life list?" she asked, her head still down. "It's 2,914." She slowly looked up from her book and said softly, "Then you've only got 2,913 to go."

About that time I glanced out the patio window and thought I saw a blue grosbeak. And I could have been right—after all, Hank's book says, they're in the neighborhood.

Tapia's Treasure

Mirrors in at least two celebrated and memorable instances have been the means and the flight to grand adventure.

The most dramatic and notable of these, of course, is Alice's passage through the looking glass and into a world of wonder. What she found there, as all children come to know, was a legion of strange new friends and an assortment of oddities.

Another adventurer was Christine, enticed to slip through a mirror with the opera's enigmatic Phantom. Christine's experiences were far less fun than Alice's. They were, indeed, quite spooky as she was taken away to the labyrinth beneath the Paris Opera House.

Nonetheless, Christine was treated to something more than ordinary.

Now I have found my own mirror. It is not framed and fashioned of polished glass, but yet it helps launch my own flight to interesting excursions.

In the depth of one night, the daughter, Maria Merced, was drawn by a mysterious light to a place on one wall.

My looking glass is the Casa de Rancho Cucamonga —better known as the Rains House—at Vineyard Avenue and Hemlock Street just north of Foothill Boulevard in Rancho Cucamonga.

Its own history and its books take me where I want to go.

I was welcomed the other day to that historic home (now part of the county museum system) by caretaker Sally Sullivan.

She, like the old casa, harbors stories of generations gone but not lost. And it is those stories that provide my adventure. During the visit in overcast and misty weather, Sally and I talked of the old Tapia treasure.

The story has been recorded, told and retold a thousand times, but it deserves to be taken from the shelf for a new telling from time to time.

Here it is: Don Tiburcio Tapia, who was born about 1800 in Los Angeles, was awarded a land grant in 1839 by the governor of California, which was part of Mexico at the time.

The grant turned out to be 13,000 acres of what is now the Cucamonga portion of Rancho Cucamonga. Senor Tapia was required by the grant to build a home on the place. He did.

And it was massive. The house, more like a fort than a home, was located on what is now Red Hill, and from what I have read, it probably was situated near what are now residences just east of Red Hill Country Club.

I would guess the Tapia house would have been in about the 8500 block of Red Hill Country Club Drive, or the street just south of there, Calle Carabe. Just a guess.

Don Tiburcio and his rancho prospered, but by the early 1840s Tapia sensed the coming onslaught of the gringo. According to legend, he feared his wealth would be lost forever. Because there were no banks as we know them, Tapia kept a considerable treasure in his house.

So he and a trusted Indian stole out in the night with a two-wheeled cart laden with riches. The story has it the two buried the treasure beneath a tree and returned to the house before dawn. The Indian was sworn by threat of a curse never to reveal the location of the treasure, and Don Tiburcio died before it was retrieved.

Years later after California had become part of the United States, and Tapia had died, his daughter and her husband occupied the famous house.

In the depth of one night, the daughter, Maria Merced, was drawn by a mysterious light to a place on one wall. What was thought to be a clue to treasure's whereabouts was located within the wall, but the clue turned out to be useless.

During the next several decades the house was virtually destroyed by treasure hunters, and much of Red Hill was dug up as well. Huge holes and caves were left in the hill.

The destroyers were all, of course, looking the gold old Tapia and the Indian buried.

The treasure was never found.

On my way home from the Rains House I noticed an old, gnarled tree in the mist across the arroyo on the eastern slope of Red Hill.

They would have had just about enough time to get to that tree and back before dawn, I thought. *I just wonder . . .*

Hondo In San Dimas

There are 230 million copies of Louis L'Amour books lying around the world, which should lead one to the reasonable assumption the man's work is popular.

This recorder of fictitious Western lore authored more than 100 books and his stories have been translated into 20 languages. The yarns, as he would describe them, have been shaped into films that have moved across motion picture and television screens for nearly 40 years.

The seemingly universal embrace of his writing leads me to wonder why I am not a devotee—a disciple of the author and his literature. But I am not.

I have read one of his books, however. It is *Hondo*.

The story is set in mean Apache country south and east of Tucson, and the protagonist is, of course, Hondo Lane, one of L'Amour's good bad guys.

The trough was dry and dusty, but it seemed to speak softly of forgotten seasons.

It was in the 1870s, and Hondo was "ridin' dispatch" for the cavalry. Hondo killed a cheat and a wimp of a man in a fair fight, then later met the unfortunate man's widow and her son on their ranch nestled near an Arizona creek bed.

Love for the Widow Lowe flowered and tasseled out, Indians became hostile, and Hondo accepted sort of a knight's appointment as protector of the little Lowe family.

In the process of carrying out that assignment he dispatched the wicked Apache Silva in a most fearful manner.

Then, on page 161 of the book, Hondo announced it was time to leave the dangerous life in Arizona and head for his ranch in California.

The place, he told the Widow Lowe, was near San Dimas.

The other day I saddled up and trotted over to San Dimas in search of Hondo's ghost.

I also wondered if some of his kin were still around.

There are a couple of "Lanes" in today's San Dimas telephone book, but because of Hondo's fictional standing I decided not to call and ask the people if they were related to an old Indian fighter.

I walked around the town's main street. Its wood plank sidewalks, shingled overhangs, a rusty water pump and old storefronts all gently picked me up and settled me back in time. I might not find Hondo, I thought, but the ghost of Gary Cooper might be a possibility.

Was that him rounding the corner at Jim's Gun and Gold Shop?

I walked by the old San Dimas railroad depot. The original burned long ago, but was rebuilt in 1934. It is now the town's tidy and comfortable Senior Citizens Center.

The day I was there Trish Cello was in charge, and several gracious ladies were painting figurines and visiting as only gracious ladies can do. The figurines were destined for the center's boutique.

Among the women there were Annie Sise, Irene Kibett and Flora Davis, who happens to be 91 years of age (perhaps she *knew* Hondo).

From there I walked across the street to the hardware store that looks as if it were a Norman Rockwell painting that in a wink became instantly and magically real.

Larry Masters was there. He owns the place, and informed me the building was constructed in 1904 and housed San Dimas' first post office. Larry's helper, Jeff Dietsch, who admitted to being an outsider from La Verne, told me the hardware store has been where it is today since 1934, when the Cushmans opened it.

I walked up the street to Ma Belle's Bakery and Deli. On the way I passed the Johnstone Block, which includes an 83-year-old building that was the site of the city's first drugstore. I also passed the old rusty pump at Exchange Place and Bonita Avenue.

The pump's trough was dry and dusty, but it seemed to speak softly of forgotten seasons.

After a sandwich at Ma Belle's I departed, leaving an age behind.

I conceded to myself I had not found a single Hondo heir, nor the old dispatch rider's ghost.

But I am almost certain I heard the jingle of his spurs along those boarded sidewalks.

Diana's World

I walked in Diana Brooks' world the other day.

It was dark there.

I was uneasy. I almost wished I hadn't come.

Why didn't I just stay in my own quarter, and not make the trip at all? I could have remained safe. Comfortable. Emerged in a normal state of things.

I could have stayed in the light. But I had, after all, asked Diana if I could join her in the tunnels and caves of the place where she is.

There is light there sometimes, but it's never lasting.

When I first learned of her, I knew we must meet. But when I called I experienced a quick, come-and-go hope she wouldn't answer the phone.

They did it with a crossbow, and buried their young victim in the woods.

After we arranged an appointment, I waited for our time together with discomforting anticipation.

I sort of twisted on it.

When we met I felt an awkwardness overtake me as a blush does. I hoped she didn't notice it.

She was a smiling, attractive woman with a certain kindness about her. But a telling intensity stole something from that look.

"What in particular do you have in mind in visiting with me?" she asked.

What do you say to a mother of a child who had been murdered? I wondered.

I knew Diana had been active in the Parents of Murdered Children organization, so I simply said, "Let's talk about your work."

"First let me tell you the difference between death and murder," she said softly. "It's one word—'violence,' and society doesn't accept that kind of death."

She said the mournful world that the murder of children creates for parents is crowded with hurt, hopelessness, hate, terror, confusion, anger and grief.

And there's more: "But one of the most difficult things to deal with," Diana said, "is coping with the stigma attached to the tragedy that is death by violence. There is this thing about murder.

"Most people view the survivors as culprits in some way. When they hear your child has been murdered they think of gangs or drugs, and wonder why you didn't raise a better kid.

"They don't realize normal people can be victims of murder, or that a little girl can be picked up at a school bus stop, beaten and killed."

Diana's son, 19, was murdered by a couple of guys whose only motive was they wanted to kill someone. They did it with a crossbow, and buried their young victim in the woods. The body wasn't found for more than a month.

That was in 1985. Diana was willing to talk to me about it, but I knew the telling of it hurt.

"People are uneasy around parents of murdered children," Diana said.

"They want to back away from you when they find out."

I remembered my own earlier apprehension, and felt silently embarrassed. A feeling of guilt crept into my thoughts.

"And the stages of grief are much different than they are for survivors of children who die but are not murdered," she said.

"At first there might not even be a body. Or the body may be mangled, or buried.

"Then there's the agony of legal procedures. They may go on for months, even years. You may find yourself at one time or another within a few feet of the person who killed your child. And you must contain yourself.

"There is other pressure among the survivors," she said. "Marriages of about 80 percent of murdered children's parents fail."

Diana, who lives in Cucamonga, was a single parent of three sons when the murder took place. The boy was her oldest.

For a couple of years she and many other surviving parents met regularly to share their tough times and to help one another.

Then the meetings slowed down and stopped.

"But the parents, especially new survivors still need each other," Diana said. "They need to talk. If they don't they'll go insane because they don't know what's normal anymore."

I could see that what she is going through is all part of bringing light to a dark world.

After a while Diana left.

And a feeling of emptiness slipped into the room.

A Day At The Pump

At one time my wife and I were accustomed to using the full-service bay when our cars needed fuel at the gas station.

The extra help was comforting.

I avoided self-service because whenever I pumped my own gas, I spent the rest of the day carrying an unwanted scent of 92 octane.

"Man, where you been?" a guy selling Winchell's donuts once asked me.

And if I decided to clean the windshield, the residual dirty water from that endeavor often found its way to my clean shirt.

I preferred to sit there in the comfort of the car and let Mike Adam and his helpers see to automotive things while I listened to *She's About As Gone As a Girl Can Get* on the country station.

My wife never considered self-service because, as she put it, the entire operation is too complex. "Besides that, the nozzle is too heavy. And it smells."

"Phew! You smell just like the Exxon Valdez just after you know what."

Then one day, while the guys were at work on my car, I looked at Mike's gasoline prices and noticed how much cheaper the fill-'er-up yourself variety can be.

That night at home I said to my wife, "We've got to start pumping our own gas."

"I'll bite, why?"

"Because it's cheaper. I figure that on one tank of gas for your car we could save almost enough to rent *The Man from Snowy River* again.

"In that case, forget it. It's a pretty dumb movie."

She doesn't like cowboy shows like I do. But she softened up a bit when I told her a few do-it-ourselves fill-ups could finance a trip to Mi Ranchito's.

"It's really not as complicated as you think," I told her. "I see women pumping their own gas all the time."

My wife surrendered to the idea, and the next Saturday morning we were off to Mike's station in the attempt to fly solo.

"Just put the credit card in this little slot," I said.

"Then what'll I do?"

"The little sign will tell you."

After a couple of abortive and frustrating efforts to get things started it was time to pick up the nozzle.

"It's too heavy," she said.

"C'mon, use both hands, I see other middle-aged ladies do it."

Wish I hadn't said that.

But in her kindness she let the comment drift off into nowhere.

"It's just not going to go in there," she said, trying to place the nozzle in the tank.

"Here, let me show you."

I couldn't get it to work.

"Just a sec. I'll go get Mike."

"The trick is to give it a little tilt just before you put it in the tank like this," Mike said, as my wife and I watched.

Mike couldn't get the thing to work either.

"It's cold out here," I said to my wife. Why don't you get in the car where it's comfortable."

I made that suggestion in an attempt to avoid the embarrassment of her watching Mike and me act like a couple of dim wits.

"It's 75 degrees," she said.

"I know, but the barometer's falling. Just get in the car."

"What do you think, Mike?" I said after she had settled in the passenger seat and picked up a magazine.

"I think something might be the matter with this sucker. Let's try it again."

More fruitless effort.

"It's not going to work, Mike."

"I know. Your wife must think we're a couple of dopes."

"You got it."

We pulled a hose from another pump.

Success this time, but I caught a splash of gasoline on my pants.

"Well, time to go," I said with a big smile as I got in the car.

"Phew! You smell just like the Exxon Valdez just after you know what."

"Never mind."

When we got home my wife handed me three one-dollar bills. "Here, this is my own money," she said, "go rent the *Man from Snowy River*."

And I did.

Now I pump gas for both of our cars.

And she doesn't even go to the station at all.

The Battle Of Chino

California's diversity, according to sagacious students of such matters, is the essence of the state's greatness.

Its variety of demographics, philosophies, politics, lifestyles, religions, topography, weather and indeed its flashing history, is a mix of the widest sort.

There is probably no place on earth of similar boundary as diverse as California. And therein, we are told, lies the basis for this state's reputation as a Land of Opportunity.

California, very simply, has it all.

Except one thing: Like the Scarecrow of Oz who so badly wanted a brain (he had adequate intelligence, but lacked a diploma) California's history is ample and colorful, but the state has no genuine military battlefield.

Wilson's command, as it turned out, was virtually without ammunition, having used it up on a hunting trip.

At least nothing like Bunker Hill, Gettysburg, Shiloh or the Alamo. But, alas, there is a site of armed conflict in California, and it's right here in this valley.

The spot marks the Battle of Chino, and all that's left of it is a four-foot brick monument on which rests a small cannon. The marker, along with a brief chiseled account of the scrap, can be found in the front yard of Chino Valley Fire Department Station 2 on Eucalyptus Avenue just west of the 71 Expressway.

I drove down there the other day in an attempt to brush the ages.

It was hot. But despite the bright sun, there was no glint from the cannon because the old weapon is gnarled and dulled out now.

The actual site of the fight is north and a bit west of the fire station on one of those slopes that rise gently north toward the grounds of Boys Republic.

Historians seem to swallow hard when describing the event as real war. In some historic accounts, writers use the words "so-called battle" when referring to the engagement.

There was, after all, but one fatality.

It was September of 1846 during the war between the United States and

Mexico, when the battle took place at the adobe ranch house (long gone now) of Isaac Williams.

His rancho covered 22,000 acres, and he came to own it by embracing Mexican citizenship and marrying a senorita of great wealth. In those days California was part of Mexico, and the Mexican government did not allow Americans to own property.

The Mexican-American War produced little combat in California. As one historian put it, Mexico "merely acquiesced to the seizure by gringos."

But there was enough indignation among local Mexicans, called Californians (or Californios) at that time, that a group led by Jose del Carmen Lugo of the San Bernardino Rancho decided to attack the Williams Rancho in Chino, which was largely occupied by gringos.

Ironically, Don Lugo was Williams' brother-in-law, which added sort of a family feud element to the whole event.

Holing up at the Williams place at the time was a company of about 20 American volunteers under command of Benjamin Wilson, another American rancher whose spread was in Jurupa.

About 80 to 100 of Don Lugo's troops, headed by Jose del Carmen, arrived at the Williams Rancho on the evening of September 26, 1846.

Wilson's command, as it turned out, was virtually without ammunition, having used it up on a hunting trip. Williams and his men also were low on bullets.

An American sent out from Williams ranch on horseback to see what Jose was up to was shot in the arm and he returned to the house on the night of the 26th, his arm broken.

The next day several shots were exchanged, and one of Jose's men was shot and killed thus creating one of the shortest casualty lists in California military history.

Finally the house was set afire by the Californios, and Williams, his family, Wilson and the rest all surrendered. Many of the Americans were arrested and taken to Los Angeles but were soon released.

The fight at Chino was over.

And then, like the Scarecrow's diploma, California received its very own battlefield.

A Visit On A Corner

He spoke to me with the help of an interpreter, but his good nature came through on its own.

He leaned against a sway-backed chain-link fence beneath a scruffy eucalyptus tree. Small bits of trash were scattered in the dirt around him.

The day was not far past dawn, and it was cool and overcast. He is very small, maybe less than 5 feet 9. He's 20 years old.

He wore a black corduroy cap, with an emblem of geese in flight stitched on the front. His shirt was mostly covered by a light jacket, and his jeans were torn open just below the right knee.

His boots were scuffed and worn.

He was quiet, and he spoke softly but was quick to smile. Sometimes he broke into a light laugh.

"Sometimes I have felt sick and wanted to go to the doctor, but I don't have enough money to go."

His name is Oscar Fernandez, and he is among those who wait at street corners for anyone who will hire them for a day's work.

Mostly he does yard chores, and irrigation repair and installation. But he paints, too.

"I will do any kind of work," he said with a bright, white and perfect smile.

His eyes were soft and had a kind look to them.

He lives in Upland, but not long ago he was on the run from war and want.

He left his native Guatemala a few years ago after winning political asylum in this country.

"Two of my uncles fought with the government and they were killed by guerrillas," he said.

"I left because there was too much war." Just about all expression left his face.

Now Oscar lives in an apartment with three other men—his brother, a cousin and a friend. The cousin and friend have jobs with a landscape maintenance crew, and the brother is a street-corner day worker like Oscar.

Oscar's mother and other brothers are still in Guatemala, and he has not been home to visit them since he left.

The fence, the eucalyptus, the trash and Oscar himself could have been the scene at a number of intersections in any Inland Valley community. But Oscar was at Arrow Highway and Grove Avenue in Upland the day we talked.

Many of the day laborers come from Central American countries such as El Salvador and Guatemala, as well as from Mexico.

There were perhaps 30 would-be workers at the corner the day I was there. Some gathered in groups of three or four. But Oscar stood alone, quiet, leaning against the fence, hands in his pockets.

He carefully watched every passing pickup or truck that slowed down.

Sometimes he and others there would raise their arms at motorists the way youngsters would raise their hands to volunteer for a coveted classroom chore.

"How long have you been coming to this corner?" I asked Oscar.

"About nine months."

"Do you find work every day?"

"Sometimes I come here and don't get anything."

"How often are you here?"

"About two or three times a week."

"How long do you wait?"

"Until about noon, then I give up. I don't do anything after that."

Oscar told me that two days a week he delivers newspaper supplements to homes in the foothill communities.

He has never had a regular, full-time job.

Have you ever been picked up here for a job that lasted longer than a day?"

"No. And I have never worked for the same boss twice."

"How much are you paid?"

"Five dollars an hour. Sometimes they try to offer us three dollars, but I don't take it. Most of the others won't work for less than five dollars."

"Do you have a favorite type of work?"

"I will do anything."

"Do you ever wait on a different corner?"

"No, always this one."

"Do you know that one city is thinking about providing a central and clean place for you and your friends to wait for jobs?"

"No, but I have heard some people want to take this corner away."

"Do you and your brother and roommates earn enough money to eat well?"

"We get by." He shrugged his shoulders.

"Do you ever go to the doctor?"

"Sometimes I have felt sick and wanted to go to the doctor, but I don't have enough money to go."

"Do you have a car?"

"No."

"What would you like to do in the future?"

"If I could, I would like to stay here, get a job and buy a house."

Then I told him I was about finished with my questions.

"Good," he said with an infectious grin, "I need to work today."

Then he waved at a man in a pickup.

I passed by the corner later in the day. A few men remained there, but Oscar was gone.

I looked at my watch and saw that it wasn't noon yet.

I hoped he had found work.

John Jamerson

You'd think that after John Jamerson learned he would never walk again he might have used himself up fighting against despair.

His world had turned cold, and an emptiness settled over him as if it were a long night.

The beginning of his life's greatest part and his hope of things to come had fallen into a state of wilt, like an old bouquet at a new grave.

He was in bed. Just stuck there with not much left to anticipate.

He had counted all the flowers on the wall.

John's dreams were gone like a candle's flame that had flickered and died in a draft's sudden gust.

He had wanted to pilot jets across the sky. Now he couldn't even stand up beside his bed.

He had wanted to pilot jets across the sky. Now he couldn't even stand up beside his bed.

An ugly tumble in the woods left his life and body broken on the rocks of a Colorado mountainside. He was paralyzed from his chest down.

And he was 15.

There were those who thought he would spend his life in bed not able to move much more of himself than his head. That was 15 years ago.

You'd think that his world would have become so small it could be shared and occupied by few others than himself.

Or that he would rarely explore beyond the boundaries of it himself. But after visiting with John the other day, I came to believe that the best part of his life did not end that day on the mountain—the best part of it had yet to come.

His world would grow to be as large as anyone's, and it would be shared by many.

After the accident, and on the way to the rest of his life he spent four days in a coma, two weeks in a semi-coma and nine months in hospitals for surgery and rehabilitation.

His education was interrupted, and he was, and is, confined to a motorized wheelchair.

But now, at 30, he is an analyst for Fontana's Engineering Department. With braces he is able to move his arms, write, type, use the telephone and he can shuffle papers with the best of us.

He lives with his parents and drives his own specially equipped car.

His smile and good looks would light a dark room.

He earned his bachelor's and master's degrees at Cal State San Bernardino in 1986 and 1992, respectively.

Now he's active, and races radio-controlled one-tenth scale dragsters, and sings karaoke at a local club. He laughed when he told me about his singing.

I carefully asked him about his goals, and he simply said he wants to learn to be as independent as possible. He works out regularly at a fitness gym.

But the young man's selflessness crept through when he said: "If I were to win the Lotto I would quit my job and do nothing more than work full time motivating young students—and I wouldn't charge anything.

"They are our future, and we must show them we are interested, and talk to them about the mistakes we made so they won't make the same ones."

He is perhaps best known around Fontana for his motivational and inspirational talks to middle school students. He urges them to stick with their education.

He said that about six months after talking to one class, a girl came to him and said, "you don't remember me, but I was in a class you talked to. And I passed because of you, and I think most of the other kids did, too."

"That's the greatest reward I could be given," John told me.

He and I agreed that adversity rearranges priorities, and sometimes places them in a new and healthy order.

He knows a lot about love, too. His voice dropped to a softness as he said, "The support and love I have received from my parents is without measure."

As we parted outside the building where he works, he wheeled away in his chair in the parking lot. The sun put a shine on his hair as it waved in the morning breeze.

He looked back over his shoulder and called out: "Come to karaoke with me sometime. I'd like to hear you sing." Then he laughed.

I thought to myself that John Jamerson probably would like to hear the whole world sing.

Ramon And The Language

When Ramon Valdez was just a boy he lived in Chino and played in the dusty streets of the barrio.

The word "barrio" probably wasn't used much in those days, for it had yet to become a popular term. But that's what is was.

His family was poor, but Ramon didn't realize it because in the Great Depression days of the '30s there was nothing much with which to compare poverty.

Everyone was poor, it seemed. There was little to covet because there was a certain sameness to everyone's lot in life. And everyone's lot was not much.

Ramon's family was close, as were most poor families of that time. The hunt for survival in those days did that to families.

When the day arrived for the children to turn in their work, Ramon had nothing to submit. He was devastated.

The boy's father was proud and hard working. Through all of the Depression he was never on welfare (or relief as they called it then), nor was he ever employed by the WPA or any other government agency. He drilled water wells throughout Southern California and was away from home much of the time.

Ramon's father was stern, but infinitely fair with his children, and he taught Ramon that if he were true to himself he would be true to everyone. The advice became the guidon that Ramon followed the rest of his life.

The mark of that paternal lesson remains on him to this day.

When Ramon was 5 years old his mother died, and he was raised by his grandparents.

Although the older couple lived in Chino, they were both born in Mexico, and were still tethered strongly to their Mexican heritage and their Mexican ways. Neither spoke English very well.

Ramon's environment rendered him bilingual when he was just a child.

His mother had spoken English well. But because she was gone from Ramon's life, and his father was away so often, the Spanish language became a dominant part of Ramon's world.

One day at grammar school, Ramon's teacher wrote "adventure" on the blackboard and instructed the youngsters in her class to write a short composition based on the word.

The essay was to be turned in a few days later.

Ramon did not know what "adventure" meant. He did not, in fact, know what "composition" meant.

He felt lost and embarrassed.

When the day arrived for the children to turn in their work, Ramon had nothing to submit. He was devastated.

The teacher kept him after school—not to punish him, but to ask him why he had not written his composition. He told her his story, and said he was sure he could have done the work if he had known what the words meant.

Ramon who has been a good friend of mine for more than 30 years, told me this story at lunch the other day while we spoke of many things.

It was that childhood incident, he said, that makes him favor bilingual education.

Clearly, he said, English is the official language in our state. It ought to be. But he said he believes bilingual education would serve as the quickest way to help kids learn the English language.

"Why should a child suffer in his studies," he said, "because he is not familiar with English and has no one at home who can help him or no one at home who cares?" "It's not fair to the children.

"It's only right to help them in school."

He said bilingual schooling should have nothing to do with ethnic relationships. All of us are, after all, Americans, Ramon said to me.

"It's something like when I was a Marine during the war. Nobody every called me a Mexican Marine. I was a U.S. Marine, just like all my buddies. "We were just trying to help one another stay alive.

"Helping each other learn is something like that." he said.

By the way, Ramon is not my friend's real name. His real name is Ruben.

Ruben Ayala.

State Senator Ruben S. Ayala.

Dogs And Me

During a break from trimming our peach tree last weekend I sat down to talk to my 11-year-old dog.

The sun felt good on my back, and the dog's fur was warm and soft. It was a good break.

Some say I keep her so that when we're caught conversing it cannot be said I am talking to myself. That's an unfair accusation because the dog is perfectly able to understand what I say. And much of what is on her mind finds its way into my own understanding.

We have been friends all of those 11 years. We're very close.

As we talked beneath the tree I was reminded of other dogs that have been part of my life.

They and I go back as far as I can remember.

There was no leash law in our little town, mostly because no one could afford to buy a leash.

The first one I recall was born before I was. He actually belonged to my brother and my father, who named him Franklin Delano Roosevelt. He was called Franklin for short.

We also had a rooster who my father told me did not wake us each morning with "cock-a-doodle-doo," but with "Vote for Roosevelt!" That should tell you something of my father's politics.

Actually, the president ripped it with my father when FDR helped orchestrate the Tennessee Valley Authority. It was then that my father became a Republican.

Meanwhile, as a kid I was certain beyond any doubt that our rooster supported the 32nd president of the United States both in voice and words.

Our dog Franklin died of old age while his namesake was still president, and we acquired another pet.

In those days you didn't buy a dog, you just sort of picked one up somewhere—from a neighbor, a school chum, or maybe you found him at the door with a smile on his face and hunger in his eye.

It was that kind of time.

Our new pet, who even as a pup displayed the propensity to sleep, was named Rip Van Winkle. We called him Rip for short.

Rip and I grew up together. And when he died, his passing gave me my first real taste of grief.

Oh, we had other dogs. But they sort of just came and went. They didn't become permanent like Franklin and Rip, and lasted just about as long as it took for them to be run over by the cars they chased.

There was no leash law in our little town then mostly because no one could afford to buy a leash.

Years later one of our three sons brought home an unwanted dog from school. I told our boys the little cockapoo was male, and they immediately named him Sgt. Mike.

That name stuck until I took the dog down to Dr. Kelber's Pet Hospital in Ontario to get shots. Seems that I was a tad wrong about the gender, Dr. Kelber said Sgt. Mike was a girl.

My sons, downplaying my lack of prowess in the field of animal husbandry, immediately renamed the new member of our family Mickey.

And she stayed that way for the next 13 years.

My buddy and neighbor, Schumway, once had a dog that lived to be 14 years old. I never really quite understood why, but the dog's name was Schumway, too.

Some time ago I was at Schumway's house helping him set gopher traps and I said to that nice Mrs. Schumway, "Aren't those two names confusing? Don't you get the two of them mixed up sometimes?"

"C'mon" Schumway said, "give me a break."

Now the Schumways are frequently visited by their 6-year-old granddaughter who owns a pup named Woody.

It's not fair to say Woody's dumb. After all, he's only 6 months old and still learning to find his dog dish. But during the Super Bowl game he knocked himself out running into the coffee table while chasing a cinnamon stick that had worked itself loose from Schumway's hot buttered rum.

"Enough reminiscing," I said to my dog. And we got back to trimming the peach tree.

Uncle Billy Rubottom

It was like *High Noon*.

Like *The Night the Lights Went Out in Georgia*.

Or the way quiet settled over the OK Corral before gunfire broke apart the stillness.

It was look-but-don't-blink time. It was time to say, "Keep your hands where I can see 'em."

Uncle Billy Rubottom squinted and looked at several armed patrons in what is now the Sycamore Inn in Rancho Cucamonga and said: "Now, gentlemen, don't make a move or I'll shoot."

Uncle Billy, whose proper name was W.W. Rubottom, was facing about 12 angry men—armed ranchers who had come to his inn to enjoy dinner and plot the lynching of Maria Merced Rains, matron of the nearby Rains Rancho.

Maria Merced, the group was convinced, was at least partly to blame for the murder of her husband, John, who was slain not long before. The killing took place in November 1862 while Rains was traveling from Cucamonga to Los Angeles.

The ranchers, all friends of the recently dispatched Rains, decided it was time to meet at the inn and plan the hanging of Rains' widow. No trial required, they figured. Uncle Billy, who also was a close friend of Rains and his wife, saw the coming of nasty business.

> *"No man or set of men can murder a woman while I'm around,"* Billy told the astonished ranchers.

He was quoted later as saying: "I made up my mind that it wouldn't happen. I'd seen enough lynching in my time, and when it came to stringing up a woman without a trial, I wouldn't stand for it in my own neighborhood."

Uncle Billy, armed with a double-barreled shotgun, and with the aid of two men named Lige and Jim, got the drop on the bad guys as the busied themselves with their plans in the inn's dining room. "No man or set of men can murder a woman while I'm around," Billy told the astonished ranchers, as he pointed both barrels at them.

The ranchers left the inn after Uncle Billy and his friends disarmed them.

Maria Merced was never threatened again. But no one was ever convicted of John Rains' murder either.

I sat in the Sycamore Inn this week and let my fantasies unwind: *Was it that long table over there where the showdown occurred?* Was that the clatter of trace and harness and the snort of a horse I just heard outside?

It surely was fantasy, because the building where the standoff took place burned decades before and was replaced by the current Sycamore Inn building in 1921 by John Klusman.

John named it the "Sycamore Hotel."

The inn is in Cucamonga's Bear Gulch along Foothill Boulevard east of Grove Avenue. Uncle Billy's name for the place was "Mountain View House," which was established as an inn and dining room in 1848.

The site of the inn also was a stopping place for Juan Batista de Anza and his band of explorers in 1774.

I remember it best when it was operated by the Hinrichsen family, who took over the inn in 1939. I must have been greeted a hundred times by Vern Hinrichsen over the distance of many years. The torch of ownership was ultimately passed by the Hinrichsens, and patrons are now served by owner Reggie Sellas.

Among Reggie's employees who see to it that meals are right are George Chavez and Tom Cincotta.

Bear Gulch is the true name of the swirl of land that spreads out from the southern slope of Red Hill where the inn is located. If a visitor looks closely enough he can see a statue of a small bear in front of the inn at the base of a huge sycamore tree.

The statue was placed there in 1932 by the Native Daughters of the Golden West. Its plaque defines the area as "Bear Gulch," and is dedicated to the "memory of California Pioneers."

The inn and the bear are located near the still-standing Rains House. The house is where Maria Merced might have spent a quiet evening 130 years ago, unaware men nearby were plotting to hang her.

Perhaps she did not know that it was Uncle Billy Rubottom's courage and double-barreled showdown that saved her life that night.

Puerto Penasco

We returned last week from the latitudes of shrimp, shell and sea where we had gone to seek peace. It was there. And having found it, we stayed several days.

The stretch of white sand on the beaches of Puerto Penasco rolled out against gulf waters that began each morning with a deep blue welcome to the new day.

By evening the sea fell silent and turned copperish and flat.

We were challenged to believe it was really water out there and not some giant layer of warm color that Mother Nature had set in place to help bring quiet to day's end.

At this time of year the shores of Puerto Penasco, on the Sonoran coast of Mexico, are mostly empty. Only a gringo or two could be seen walking along the expanse of sand and shell.

From time to time a local would shuffle out, pantlegs up, to rake near the surf for something that possibly would sell.

From time to time a local would shuffle out, pantlegs up, to rake near the surf for something that possibly would sell.

And sometimes there were no people at all along the great sweep of beach.

The shoreline's crescent forms a shallow bay and port that harbors the little town's fleet of shrimp boats. The rusty vessels are part of Puerto Penasco's No. 1 industry.

We visited cantinas, little restaurants, fish markets, shops, and the sheltered fleet as well as settlements around Cholla Bay.

Everywhere we traveled I longed for the ability to speak the local language. The grace, hospitality and friendliness of the people of Puerto Penasco radiates from their smiles and their native speech.

Their mood seems to be in a perpetual state of good. When they are obliged to speak English so they can converse with foreigners such as I, something of the romance of it all slips away.

I took with me on the trip a small Spanish-English dictionary. And the possibility of embarrassment did not slow me down in my struggle to speak to the natives in their own tongue while reading from the book as we spoke.

This practice worked particularly well at JJ's Cantina at Cholla Bay. We had gone there in hunt of sand dollars and to enjoy an afternoon cerveza on JJ's veranda.

While my companions explored the bay at low tide, I talked to Sanchez in the cantina. He was watching *Carmen on Ice* on a small TV behind the bar. The production offered the entire opera, with full orchestra and chorus. It was being performed by Mexican skaters.

My little language book kept me in beer and sketchy conversation about the misfortunes of the ice-skating Spanish Gypsy. My friends returned before Carmen's demise.

The last pages of my little dictionary contain phrases rather than just words and definitions. I was drawn to this speech simply because its cadence and tone seem somehow kinder than one word spoken at a time in a jerky attempt to wander about in the Spanish language.

For instance, I think, *Usted es muy amable* has nice music to it. My little book tells me it means "You are very kind." I used that one a lot.

I committed several phrases to memory, choosing the ones that sounded especially pleasing. Their meaning was more or less immaterial to me. Like, *Puede venderme sellos correo?*—"Can you sell me some stamps?" My use of this phrase resulted in my returning home with an abundant surplus of Mexican postage.

One evening we walked to a cantina with companions Millie Holmes and Barbara Biane, both from back home in the Inland Valley. After the drink orders were taken I smiled and said to the waiter, *"Esta funda no se ve limpia."* I thought the phrase had a nice ring to it.

"Do you know what you just said?" Millie asked, as the waiter left our table.

"I'm not really sure."

"You told the man the pillowcase doesn't look clean."

"Uh, oh."

Millie told me later she thought our margaritas tasted funny.

"I think," Barbara said quietly, "I know why."

Lucille

One look at Lucille Beekman's bathing suit and you would guess she'd sink if she ever wore it swimming.

If s made of wool, and it's long and bulky.

It's not on *Sports Illustrated's* 10 most wanted list.

I don't think Jantzen designed it. And it's very old.

Lucille doesn't use the water wear any longer because it's hanging in the Chaffey High School Alumni Association's campus office in Ontario.

It is displayed there as a simple mark of Lucille's time as a Chaffey student.

She began her freshman year there 82 years ago.

I visited with Lucille the other day, and she spoke of the bathing suit with the same keen humor she used to describe her life and times in this valley since her arrival here in 1908.

She prefers to talk about what has been right with her life than what has been wrong with it.

Her chuckles and quick wit invite you along to see the best in everything. So you go.

Lucille doesn't simply tolerate life, she takes charge of it. Wherever she goes she takes her own brand of vibrancy with her.

If you want to be grumpy, don't go to see her—she'll ruin your plans.

"She turned 96 last Friday," said a friend and visitor, Marian Nelson. "And we partied all week," Lucille quickly added. But her wink and grin gave away a tad of exaggeration in the boast.

"People always ask me how I have lived so long, and why my health is so good. Well, I have enjoyed good health all right, but for no particular reason I can think of. "I never was diet mad like people are today. I eat anything I want. I never had a glass of milk in my life."

Lucille is small in stature but tall in good nature and spark. She'd rather laugh than complain, and she prefers to talk about what has been right with her life than what has been wrong with it.

When I asked her how much she weighs, she smiled and said she wouldn't tell me. "But I'm trying to get back up to 100, and I'm pretty close."

I didn't mention it to her, but I wondered which would come first, 100 pounds or 100 years. She'll make both, I thought.

Lucille's father was a grocer, and the family moved to Cucamonga when Lucille was 9. She graduated from Chaffey High in 1917. She was out of high school for two years while caring for her ailing sister and mother. In the early years she drove a horse and buggy to school, and later she rode the first red cars part way.

Her husband, Clifford, was a citrus rancher, and sometimes worked in the groves for others.

"He was paid 85 cents an hour," Lucille said. "And that was for both himself and his team."

Later the couple purchased a 10-acre grove and house on Base Line in Cucamonga. "We paid $11,500 for both the grove and the house in 1930, and had it paid off by 1942."

Although Lucille was trained as a surgical nurse at San Antonio Community Hospital, she only worked for a year. "I never had a paying job after that."

A son and three daughters were born to Lucille and Clifford, who died in 1981.

Last Saturday Lucille was the oldest among a couple of hundred members of the Chaffey Alumni Association who gathered for a picnic on Chaffey's North Quad.

There was food, and good times.

Jack Mercer and some former Chaffey band members made picnic music. The pep squad danced.

During the festivities, Ed Berryman, association president, announced that some years ago Lucille had lost her 1917 yearbook, *Fasti*. It was a sad loss.

Somehow Ed had obtained a copy of another one, and he gave it to Lucille during the picnic. People clapped. Under Lucille's picture in that 1917 *Fasti*, were the words: "I have a heart for every joy."

Saturday evening after the picnic, friends and family took Lucille out to a restaurant. She ate a steak dinner.

"Remember, I'm trying to get back up to 100."

This Town's Name Just Won't Die

Putting an end to Narod is like trying to kick the cat out of the house on a cold night.

Narod won't die.

It is a once proud community in our midst that seems to have had immortality thrust upon it. Like Rocky, it keeps getting up off the canvas.

If you can believe Narod gave up its place in history then you can believe John Paul Jones left the bridge and hid.

Or Babe couldn't hit.

Narod's pulse continues well beyond the time of its presumed expiration.

How do I know? Because the few occasions on which I have mentioned that old community in my work we have received calls, letters, faxes, smoke signals and one phone call from E.T.

The originators of these contacts are folks who know something of Narod and its early days and are willing to share their recollections.

To them, the town is as much a part of their past as a cold bottle of Nehi.

To them, the town is as much a part of their past as a cold bottle of Nehi. Or Floyd Young's fruit frost reports on early morning radio.

In the minds of most people Narod, which never was an incorporated city, no longer exists because it has been absorbed by real towns. But when there was a Narod it was located in the area surrounding Central Avenue and State Street, hard by the tracks of the Union Pacific and Southern Pacific railroads.

It sort of floated there between Chino and Monte Vista (now Montclair) and was a Union Pacific whistle-stop, a cluster of homes, an old hotel and a couple of packing sheds.

It was well known as Narod as late as the 1950s.

Thanks to people such as Charles Balding, Earl and Renee Newman, Jim Maples, Gene Skiles, Peter Sehiavoni and William "Tex" Hartley, I now know more about Narod than ever before.

I have learned of Three-Fingered Jack, Sunsweet, bootleggers and "that kid from Narod."

Earl and Charles both called to tell me that Narod was not always called that. At one time it was known as Sunsweet, a name given to the area by the railroad. Obviously Sunsweet died a quicker death than Narod.

Then I learned from Tex that Narod was named for railroad official A.E. Doran, whose last name spelled backwards is, what else, Narod.

Gene, whose family moved to Narod in the 30s when he was just a youngster, told me he rode his bike or walked to school in Chino in those days.

His Chino school chums always called Gene "that kid from Narod." That name for him, over the years, was ultimately shortened to "Narod." And that has been his first name ever since.

It is, in fact, where the one-time popular Chino restaurant got its name. Mr. Gene "Narod" Skiles opened and operated the eatery for many years.

When he was a kid, Gene lived in a Narod apartment house in what was once a hotel near Central and State Street. He said he knew a man in the community named Three-Fingered Jack, who, I assume, had only three fingers on one hand and sported a conventional number of digits on the other.

Jack lived in a cave, Gene said and worked in nearby groves irrigating and smudging.

Earl Newman, who well remembers Narod in the 1920s, said that during Prohibition days, those who succumbed to the need of drink would contact a certain man in Narod.

He was the only bootlegger around. The bootlegger took his thirsty customers' money then gave them directions to where a bottle could be found.

"He kept his bottles in a grove at an intersection a bit north of Narod," Earl told me.

"He would tell us to count 12 rows from the intersection then go 18 trees into the grove, and our bottle would be sitting against the tree trunk. "By golly, it was always there."

And the calls about Narod keep coming to me. Recently I decided to test the endurance of the name, and one day while I was out of town I phoned home for the information operator.

"What city, please?" the operator asked. "Narod," I said with a smirk.

"OK, what number?" she asked.

I give up.

Seely

To a small cadre of his friends, Don Seely is known as a man about town.

I'm not certain he knows that. The title is not derogatory. It is, in fact, brushed with a-not-so-thin coat of dignity.

And it took some time to earn. Don is a retired barber who once cut hair in the step-down shop at the old, and now burned, Orange Hotel in Ontario.

After many years there, he moved to Euclid Avenue where Red Wellborne, prince of Ontario barbers, passed his crown to the younger, but no less colorful, Don Seely.

It was in that shop, which was a scene Norman Rockwell would have been inclined to preserve, that Don played out the rest of his career.

One of his partners in the shop was Curly Allsup, who was noted for being the father of the girl (Dee, a Chaffey High School graduate) who married author Joseph Wambaugh.

> *The weight of his recent hatred and his fleeting thoughts of committing homicide crowded his mind.*

If the shop looked Rockwellian, so did much of its clientele. It was a place where nothing too stern dared enter.

For example, I went in there one Friday afternoon to have my shoes glossed at the shoeshine stand.

"He stepped out," Don said, noting the shoeshine guy's absence.

Deciding to wait for him to return, I picked up a *U.S. News and World Report*. I sort of skimmed the magazine and then gathered up another.

About a half-hour passed by the time I had partly read the second magazine. Neither Don nor I talked during that time. No one else was in the shop. Later I looked nervously at my watch and said to him, "When did he leave, anyway?"

"Tuesday." He said it without expanding on the comment.

Don is like that.

Recently his imported car developed some awful malady, so he placed it in the care of an independent mechanic specializing in foreign cars.

Just a minor fix was necessary, Don was told.

When he picked up the car later and asked the guy what the charge would be, he was told $260.40.

The news registered about 6.8 on the Seely Scale. The blood drained from his head. He asked for a chair. A glass of water would be helpful.

"Will you say that again real slow," Don said.

"Two-hundred-and-sixty-dollars and-forty cents," the mechanic said with method but no emotion.

Although silent about it, Don was furious. He could not believe that it cost that much to replace a part he could hold between his thumb and forefinger. He was so angry he didn't speak, fearing something awful would come of it.

There was much hate in him. Real hate.

He paid the mechanic, but he would have preferred to have killed him, figuring he had been soundly swindled.

Later and still seething in silence, Don called the service department of the authorized dealer for the type of car he had repaired.

"I've got this li'l ol' part I can hold between my thumb and forefinger," he told the guy. "It needs to be replaced. What will it cost?"

Then he described the part in greater detail.

"Just a sec." the guy said. "I'll look it up."

He was off the phone less than a minute, and when he returned he told Don, "The charge on that job will be $347.00."

Thanks," Don said, and hung up.

Feelings of guilt overwhelmed Don.

The weight his recent hatred and his fleeting thoughts of committing homicide crowded his mind. For he now realized his mechanic had actually saved him $86.60. So he left his house, got in his car, drove down to Winchell's on Euclid and bought a dozen doughnuts.

Then he traveled to the shop of the mechanic who repaired his car.

Don walked up to the guy who was half gone under the hood of a sports car.

"Here," Don said, as the mechanic straightened up, wiping his hands on a rag. "I want you to have these."

"That's nice," the guy said. "How come the doughnuts?"

"Never mind," Don said, satisfied the cycle of atonement for his dreadful sin was now complete. "Just eat 'em."

Then he left to run more man-about-town errands.

Don is like that.

The Floods

We now have three Inland Valley floods to talk about.

Besides the one from which all of us are still wringing out our socks, there were the famous floods of 1969 and 1938. And if you care to go back far enough you can find a fourth—a pretty soppy storm pounded through here in 1904, washing a considerable amount of desert dirt and debris clear out of the county.

And now we have what will be forever known as "The Flood of '93."

Which of these natural disasters was the worst?

To try to find the answer I visited the Ontario Library. Helping me in my hunt for old and angry water were Joanne Boyajian, head of adult services; Alice Camargo, receptionist; and Roseann Ochoa, circulation clerk, all of whom were kind and patient.

My window to soggy history was a look at old newspaper accounts of the storms.

Upland High School became a virtual refugee camp, and crowds were fed by the Red Cross and Salvation Army workers.

I disregarded the flood of '04, because there were so few people and structures in the valley then it is impossible to compare the damage and havoc of 1904 to the wreckage that came later.

I limited my study to the floods of 1938, 1969 and 1993. Because there are so many variables at work, it is difficult to draw direct comparisons of ruin wrought by these storms.

In 1938, for instance, there was no San Antonio Dam or network of flood-control channels, so the flood runoff was more ravaging than it was in later years.

But there were fewer homes and people to suffer at the hands of the storm in 1938.

So the comparison is challenging. Nonetheless, I will be bold and state that the 1969 flood was the biggy of the three.

Although there was less rain recorded in the 1969 storm (12.5 inches) than has been recorded this month (13.87 inches) there was greater damage in '69.

What made the 1969 storm so devastating was one particular downpour during the two weeks of wet weather. It came January 24 through 26, and dumped more than 8 inches in Ontario and more than 9 inches in Alta Loma.

Property loss was set at $20 million (some said it was more), but in today's dollars that could be five times that amount, considering one could buy a pretty nice home in those days for $17,000.

The 1993 storm damage probably will be less than $30 million, and the death toll may not reach five.

Miraculously there were only two local deaths reported in 1969. The *Los Angeles Times* reported on January 29, 1969, that 92 people died in the storm throughout all of Southern California, and eight others were missing.

Locally, eight bodies were recovered in the 1938 10-inch storm, but nearly 200 died throughout Southern California. The rain of '38 was bad. Some old-timers still insist it was the worst.

But it was the property damage and high drama in '69 that help give the storm its nasty reputation. Thousands of homes were damaged or lost in the flood, and more than 2,000 residents had to be evacuated from their northeast Upland homes.

Many were plucked from rooftops by U.S. Marine helicopters. The evacuees were housed in schools, homes, churches and wherever else they could find safety. Upland High School became a virtual refugee camp, and crowds were fed by the Red Cross and Salvation Army workers. Many remained homeless well after the storm subsided.

City water turned bad, roads were closed, schools were shut down, and it took weeks for any kind of normalcy to return.

Mt. Baldy Village was isolated—bridges were washed away and the road was cut in two at many places.

The Buckhorn Lodge was virtually destroyed, half of it left hanging over the creekbed that roaring runoff water had widened to several hundred feet.

A lake 54 feet deep formed behind Prado Dam.

That was the flood '69. The granddaddy of them all.

Ginger

My wife went away for a week-long family visit recently, leaving my 10-year-old dog and me to batch.

The dog and I are bad for each other. We watched more ESPN than we usually do—serious stuff like tractor pulls.

And at every opportunity we viewed all the pre-1945 cowboy shows we could find on TV. The dog and I weren't lucky enough to encounter a Hopalong Cassidy movie, but Joel McCrea showed up a couple of times.

Like the television viewing, our meals shifted out of the norm. Peanut butter was in, Brussels sprouts and jicama were out. The forbidden menus ranged from cold leftover scallop potatoes with catsup for breakfast to sardines right out of the can.

My wife telephoned toward the end of her stay suggesting I meet her in Encinitas so I could join in her visit on the weekend. So I decided to take Amtrak down to Del Mar just south of Encinitas

I caught the train in Fullerton. As I settled into my window seat a bubbly young woman asked if she could sit on the aisle next to me.

"Sure."

She wore a broad and pleasing smile and she was as full of life as a Disneyland carousel.

She wore a short, tight skirt and a big, broad and pleasing smile. Her knit blouse was tight like her skirt, and she was as full of life as a Disneyland carousel.

The lethargy I picked up waiting for the train earlier swiftly vanished, and I found myself laughing along with my new and carefree companion.

I soon learned her name was Ginger, and it was the first day of her vacation. "So look out, here I come!" she warned. And she laughed again.

"Want a beer?" she asked me. "There's a snack bar in the next car. I'll go get in line."

"Why not," I said.

"Ain't this better than working?" she said laughing as she left to line up at the snack bar. She was back in a while with three beers. She handed me one and said, "This one's for you." She noticed me looking at her two beers and said, "Hate to stand in line, ya know."

We talked and laughed a lot, mostly about the restaurant where she worked.

"Hi, Ginger," said a guy later as he sat down across the aisle. "Want a beer?" He returned to his feet and headed for snack bar. "Sure," she called after him. "And mud in your eye. Ha ha."

Then she turned to me and said, "That's Ron. He's a meat cutter. Great guy. Has a store by my apartment. Real friendly."

Ron returned and gave Ginger two beers without comment. "Bet he hates to stand in line," I said. "You got that right. Me too. I just hate it," she said.

Then we all talked for a while. And laughed. Ginger said she was headed for Del Mar to pick up her sister for a trip to Mammoth.

"We're going to get into nature and catch fish and stuff. Live it up a little too," she said, laughing.

I got up to stretch my legs, and she asked me if I would please fetch her some beer. When I returned with two beers for her she said, "That's great. I hate standing in line." "Me too," Ron said from across the aisle. And they both chuckled.

We talked some more as the cliffs of San Clemente went by. There was a lot of laughter, and Ginger wondered if Japanese soldiers ever got as far as these cliffs during World War II. Ron said he didn't think so.

Then finally it was time to leave the train.

Later while my wife and I were putting my bag in the trunk of her car at the Del Mar station, Ginger leaned out the window of a passing van and shouted, "Bye, hon. it was great being with you!"

Her blonde hair was flowing in the summer wind.

I wish she hadn't done that.

With a ton of quiet patience my wife simply asked. "Who was that?"

"That's Ginger."

Then acting a bit flustered and not being able to think of anything else, I said, "She hates standing in line."

The Chaffey House

During a rare spring weather day in March I shared lunch with Lydia Kremer on Mimi's patio in Upland. The sun, which had spent much of the month elsewhere, had returned. It was bright, and it gave us some friendly warmth.

Lydia lives in Rancho Cucamonga, and she, like many of her neighbors, is a relative newcomer to that foothill community.

During our lunch, Lydia described her love affair with her new hometown as well as her appetite for stories and events that have preceded her here. The valley's history calls her as it does many of her neighbors. Accounts of the past, she says, are rich.

The cast in the valley's historic drama includes the work and times of American Indians, Spaniards, explorers, Mexican dons, pioneers, soldiers, stagecoach riders, early day developers, ranchers and steelworkers.

The first electric light bulb to glow on the West Coast was placed in the Chaffey home on December 4, 1882.

Rancho Cucamonga sits atop all this adventure.

It doesn't seem long ago that in this community Uncle Billy Rubottom operated the Mountain View Inn, which is now called the Sycamore Inn. It is still at the original location on Foothill Boulevard east of Grove Avenue.

During the Civil War, Uncle Billy kept the considerable local population of Confederate sympathizers happy by serving good Southern cooking.

Nowadays, Jim Clark, a valley resident for 65 years, believes there are many people in our valley who are not aware of what has gone before.

Jim's been around these parts so long that he might regard anyone who has lived here less than 30 years as someone who is just be passing through.

He lives in Etiwanda, and has been best known in recent years for his No. 1 dedication—the restoration of the home of George Chaffey, who with his brother, William, founded the Etiwanda and Ontario Colonies in the 1880s.

The home, already well along toward restoration, is on Etiwanda Avenue adjacent to the Etiwanda Community Church north of Base Line. It was moved there in 1985 from its original location on Etiwanda between Highland Avenue and Summit.

The fact that Chaffey resided where he did might give weight to the theory that Etiwanda, not Ontario, was Chaffey's original choice for the primary settlement in the valley.

Chaffey bought the house from Joseph Garcia in 1881. Garcia built it seven years earlier.

It wasn't until some time later that the Chaffey brothers founded the Ontario Colony with its famous Euclid Avenue.

The Chaffey home's fame transcends its relationship to the man who occupied it.

The first long-distance telephone hook-up in the world was established in 1882 when Chaffey extended a line between his Etiwanda house and San Bernardino.

The first electric light bulb to glow on the West Coast was placed in the Chaffey home on December 4, 1882.

Chaffey produced electricity with hydro-electric power. A wheel was turned by water tumbling out of the canyon from the north of Chaffey home.

The 118-year-old Chaffey house has been reconstructed, but restoration of its interior remains to be done. Ultimately the place will be a museum surrounded by a small orange grove and a hedgerow of eucalyptus trees.

A rose garden will be a part of the landscape. There are other landmarks throughout the Inland Valley, but probably few people would challenge the idea that a restored and healthy Chaffey home would be the most significant among them.

After all, if there really is a Father of Our Cities, it would be George Chaffey.

Although Chaffey, well known, for founding Ontario, never lived in that city. But he is buried there.

Meanwhile, Etiwanda can always claim to be the home of the great engineer and genius. It has the house to prove it.

And that house will certainly beckon those who like history—such as my lunch companion, Lydia Kremer, and her neighbors.

A Word That's Gone With The Wind

Recently I wrote, in a rather oblique manner, that winds, sweeping out of the canyons to rake the valley with particular ferocity once were called "Santana winds."

Innocently, and with no ill intent, I stirred an old fire.

Those canyon blasts, usually hot and fierce, today are universally referred to as "Santa Ana winds."

The transition between the use of those two terms did not come without conflict. Perhaps even some pain.

A deep line was (and still is) drawn between the people who preferred one reference and those who chose the other.

Flatlanders participating in the debate could, and would, display rocking emotions in defending their stand as well as the definition of the word to which they were so devoted.

The Daily Report clung to "Santana" until the band played Good Night, Sweetheart.

The argument was not limited to San Bernardino County residents, who usually absorb the first hit of the ornery winds.

Like the wind itself, the lively dialogue rushed across all of Southern California.

I was reminded of the old push and pull of it all last week when I received a letter from Happi Moore of Pomona. She wrote: "I love the fact that you know that our high winds are 'Santanas,' not 'Santa Anas' and I keep wondering why the TV medium reporters are either unthinking or uncaring of the facts."

Happi's comment resurrected memories of the old war. The embers of the fire I thought, still glow. Many say that the fact is "Santana," or "devil winds," were the terms originally applied.

My guess is early Spaniards or Mexicans were the first Californians to refer to the winds as "Santanas." Who knows for sure?

As out-of-state immigrants began to saturate Southern California in the middle part of this century, "Santana" slowly became mutilated by the new arrivals' speech.

And Happi is correct. Television news readers contributed lightly to the beginning of the end of that romantic word, "Santana."

Traditionalists argued, with apparent logic, that the winds had nothing to

143

do with the city of Santa Ana, Orange County, the great general or the saint herself, and therefore "Santa Ana winds" was—and is—a term founded on nothing at all.

Newcomers, according to the old-timers who puffed with great righteousness, just didn't know what they were talking about.

But there are some old stalwarts who argue that "Santa Ana" was, indeed, the historical and accurate description of the winds. Again, who knows?

The tilt of all this took on a rather pesky slant when the news media—both print and broadcast—could not make up their minds.

The time arrived when newspapers and television people consistently contradicted themselves in the undisciplined use of both terms that described the wild winds that funnel through the canyons and across the flat of the valley.

The news media believed reason would be served if they used only one the terms, not both.

It soon became evident that "Santa Ana" was gradually becoming the apparent survivor of the tug between the two. And some news organizations officially embraced it in order to bring consistency to their reports.

"Santana" was on its way to oblivion. The *Los Angeles Times*, The *Associated Press* and *United Press International* news bureaus in Los Angeles all finally announced that "Santana" was out and "Santa Ana" was in. They dumped, what some will forever claim, was the original and historic term.

The final coffin nail was placed when the National Weather Bureau dropped "Santana" from its reports, forecasts and statistics.

The Daily Report (now the *Inland Valley Daily Bulletin*) clung to "Santana" until the band played *Good Night, Sweetheart*. But 20 or so years ago the term "Santana winds" left its pages forever. That is until I mentioned it several days ago.

That's what generated Happi's letter. I suppose the dispute may still be glowing somewhere there in the ashes. But the flame is mostly gone.

Diamond Bar

The morning dew on the ranch was so heavy you could smell it.

A presence of a scattered herd of white face cattle interrupted the green expanse of the winter hills. And the sun worked until the dew lost its glint and disappeared until another day.

From a distance the cattle seemed not to move at all, frozen in place as if they were part of a pretty picture.

But a closer glance revealed that they occasionally stopped their grazing and lifted their heads to look around. Sniff the breeze.

There was nothing there on those hills except the cattle, grass, oak trees, a ranch house hidden by eucalyptus, the few people who ran the place and a cowboy or two.

It was quiet.

It was the Diamond Bar Ranch in 1950, more or less hidden from the rest of the world. A ring of hills isolated it, cutting it off from Pomona on the north and Brea on the south.

> Not counting the cows and the few who worked the ranch, the population of Diamond Bar was 0—zero.

A narrow, two-lane road meandered north and south through the ranch, and I sometimes drove the length of the valley just to remind myself that the whole world was not paved over.

There were no houses or other buildings in that small valley, except the ranch house.

It could have been called "Tranquillity."

The population of the United States in 1950 was 151 million. And not counting the cows and the few who worked the ranch, the population of Diamond Bar was 0—zero.

I hope this place never falls to progress. Please, commercialism, don't come, I would say to myself.

Today the population of the nation is 250 million, and 54,000 of them live and work in the city of Diamond Bar, a town that rolled over the ranch.

In one place, the freeway that thunders through the valley is at least eight lanes wide.

Commercialism did, indeed, come.

Now the largest development in the city's history is being considered.

And about 200 of Diamond Bar's residents have collected their vigor to oppose the commercial venture that would bring 650 new residents to the city.

A line of conflict is being drawn in the valley, and is resulting in a test between the will of those who hold to the land and city officials and developers who want Diamond Bar to expand.

There is a sense of righteousness on both sides. It runs so deep that the gray color of compromise is apt to be painted over by a black-and-white approach to things.

One side calls the other "no-growthers" who are not of the real world, and describe them as those who already have their houses on the hill and want to keep everyone else out.

That same side asserts that all 54,000 residents, including the 200 opponents of the new plan, once lived somewhere else and were themselves reckoned with as intruders in the valley.

On the other side of the debate, developers are characterized as greedy folk who care little for the land, and less for those who want to protect it.

Somewhere between these poles of thought must be common ground.

Most of the 54,000 who moved in while the ranch was moving out are decent enough folk. So are the 200 who don't want to see one more oak fall to ax or dozer.

God bless 'em.

But without developers, remember, those 54,000 people would not have homes in which to live.

The real invader of the land, throughout the nation as well as in our own valley, is simply the absolute need of a growing population to have places in which to live, work and go to school.

The 99 million people in the United States who were not here in 1950 have to live somewhere. It's a basic truth.

There's a temptation to embrace "anywhere but here" as a solution.

But is that answer right?

Is it fair?

Was it fair 15 years ago?

Was it fair 40 years ago?

In the end, the ranch could not be saved. Neither could the trees, the cattle or the cowboys or the quiet mornings.

But the future can be handled with care and grace.

Perhaps the people who live where the ranch once was will find the grace and apply the care.

What's In Upland's Name?

When Bill Romero first introduced himself to me he sort of mumbled his last name, and I didn't get it.

"How do you spell that?" I asked.

"B-I-L-L."

At that instant I knew Bill was my kind of guy. And we've been friends ever since.

Not long ago he asked me if I knew Upland was once called North Ontario.

He also asked if I knew why and when the community came to be the city of Upland.

"I know a lot of things around here used to be named something else," I told him, "but I don't really know how Upland got its start."

A few days later someone else asked me the same question.

Then I received a note from Isabel Whitney suggesting I look into Upland's beginning.

I felt as if the question about Upland was spreading like a computer virus.

I knew it was time for me to visit LaVera Miller, the head lady at Ontario Library's Ontario Colony Room.

She handed me *Dreamer and Dwellers*, a book by Bernice Bedford Conley that records the history of Ontario and its neighbors.

> **If it had been successful there would be no Upland today, and Ontario would now have a population of nearly 200,000.**

Author Conley's account of Upland's origin traces a virtual war between Ontario, North Ontario and Upland of considerable proportions.

Here are some interesting up-front facts:

—Both Ontario and Upland tried municipal incorporation as one city in 1885, but it didn't work.

—Upland approved incorporation not once, but twice—the first time in 1902 and again in 1906.

—Parts of what are now Upland once lay within the city limits of Ontario.

Here's the history:

North Ontario was laid out and named in 1887. It had its own post office and was distinctly separate from Ontario.

In 1888 an election was held to incorporate Ontario and North Ontario into one city. The incorporation failed.

If it had been successful there would be no Upland today, and Ontario would now have a population of nearly 200,000.

In 1891 voters approved incorporation of Ontario, excluding North Ontario, because it had fallen into economic slumber, and Ontario did not want to be encumbered by that.

By 1895 North Ontario began to prosper, so Ontario attempted to annex it with the idea of embracing the community's boom and taking the Santa Fe Railroad into its own boundaries.

Two annexation elections failed that year.

On April 14, 1901, another annexation was attempted by Ontario, but this time the boundaries excluded North Ontario land owned by those who voted against annexation six years earlier.

The annexation was approved, so a portion of what is now Upland found itself within the city of Ontario. A year later, however, legal action was filed against Ontario in an attempt to annul the annexation.

The petitioners also sought to secede North Ontario from Ontario and to incorporate the community as a city.

The petitioners of that session changed the name of the community to Upland. In anticipation of the incorporation, Upland was officially named on April 22, 1902.

The next month residents cast 113 votes to incorporate Upland, and six voted against.

But get this: the county Board of Supervisors (bowing to incorporation opponents) declared the election invalid.

Incorporation proponents took the whole matter to the courts, and for the next five years the two communities haggled over boundaries, annexations and incorporation.

Then in 1906, a new incorporation election was held and on May 5, residents voted 183 to 19 to make Upland a city.

It stuck. And all of Upland was put back into one piece.

So the cities of Ontario and Upland went to incorporation polls four times: once together in 1888, Ontario alone in 1891, Upland in 1902 in a voter-approved incorporation that died in litigation, and finally Upland in 1906.

So there you have it, B-I-L-L, Isabel and others.

And thank you, LaVera Miller.

Kelly's Mine And Mountain

About this time each year I hear a quiet call to the San Gabriels, that great wall of cliff, timber and stream that is our mountain neighbor.

I like the way the 10,000-foot giant range towers over us with its own kind of majesty, serving as sort of a trademark for our whole valley. The range, with its ragged ridges, has a million personalities, its color ever changing with the fickle moods of sun and season.

There are times in winter when the mountain snow is turned a wondrous pink by day's late light.

Pink snow? You bet.

Then on clear winter days the range juts up to tangle with the sky, forming a jagged and sharp encounter between the whitest white and the bluest blue.

> *There are times in winter when the mountain snow is turned a wondrous pink by day's late light.*

In another time of year, autumn rain sometimes brings an early green to the range's chaparral. Of course, midsummer often turns our mountains blue.

And during the toughest of times, the San Gabriels are not there at all, taken from us by a mix of haze, marine air and the residue of man's hurry. Are the mountains really there? we ask.

But spring is a special time for me because it works away at winter snow, taking drifts, ice and pure cold off the mountain so that we flatlanders can wander its canyons, creeks and summits.

It is time when I think of backpacking years ago to Kelly's Camp, that historic settlement cupped in woods not far from Ontario Peak's north and shadowed slope.

It's a five-mile hike up there. The walk is not for sissies, but the rewards are lasting.

It can be reached from a trail head in Cucamonga Canyon, just a whoop north of Mt. Baldy Village.

Kelly's is only a trail camp now, but when I traveled there with sons and companions, most of Kelly's digs remained.

Back in the teens he mined there, and built himself a lumber mill, a lodge, cookhouse, a few sleeping cabins and a water well with a real bucket, pulley and rope.

His equipment, engines, lumber and supplies were all hauled up the canyon by horses and pack mules.

Although Kelly was gone by the time I made my first visits there, his camp survived, and we hikers reveled in many nights of song, fire and good company protected from night's chill by what was left of Kelly's buildings.

It was in those times that old mountaineer Kilgore Collier taught my young sons to respect the woods.

In the 1920s, Kelly's Camp (sometimes his name can be found spelled "Kelley") was a popular spot for outings by families and friends.

Now I have heard from a thoughtful John Boal of Upland, who was kind enough to send me a copy of a Camp Baldy Co. brochure listing the vacation and stage schedule for the village's 1926 season.

The brochure lists activities available at what is now Mt. Baldy Village. It boasts of cabins, tents, hiking, horseback riding, free dancing (every night except Sunday), swimming pool, tennis courts, bowling alleys and a soda fountain.

Vacationers were charged 76 cents for breakfast, a dollar for lunch and supper, except Sunday dinner, which went for $1.60. Two people could rent a cabin for $30 per week or a tent for $12.

The brochure, obviously aimed at the Los Angeles market, informed prospective guests they could leave the L.A. Pacific Electric Depot, travel to Upland on the train, then transfer to a stage for a jostling ride up San Antonio Canyon to the village. It took nearly three hours to make the trip, and the fare was $3.75.

Those yesteryears must have been of the sublime sort.

Of Kelly and his mine.

Of city folk aboard train and stage.

And of my own time in those ravines.

It's like a thing that beckons.

And it happens every spring.

24 Tortillas

When I am sent for tortillas I sometimes do the shopping at Nancy's Tortilleria in Pomona.

I remember when the little bakery (it was called a factory then) was a four-wall, stone, squat building just south of the main entrance to Nancy's relatively new market.
The flashing brown eyes and the sort of shy smiles of the tortilla magic makers there were as warm as the fresh goodness they prepared.

Nancy is really Jose Manuel and Teresa Vergara, who own the bakery.

The real Nancy is their 17-year-old daughter, who was about three when Jose opened the original factory.

The place was named for the little girl.

Nancy's seems to be a bit of misplaced Old Mexico—as if it drifted up here with the wind.

Having purchased my two dozen tortillas, I ventured over to Petra and Willle Lopez's El Merendero Bakery on Third Street for some bolillos and rosca.

To this day, when I walk in there I feel as if I am lost in the latitudes of Algodones down on the border.

An abundance of Spanish is spoken at Nancy's.

I do not count myself among those who regard the use of non-English in our midst as some sort of calculated affront.

I envy people who can speak in a tongue other than their own—or *my* own.

I am, unfortunately, linguistically lame—no, crippled.

My neighbor, Schumway, has chided me by saying, "You're so dumb about Spanish, you think Zapata's first name was Viva!"

Ol' Schum also has been known to accuse me of "not being able to habla much Spanish," whatever that means. Somehow it doesn't sound right.

Ginny Ferndino, my one-time travel agent in Pomona, scolded me once for asking her how to say "OK" in Japanese.

The other day my wife sent me for a couple of dozen tortillas. That simple request created an interesting challenge, because I almost always buy tortillas a dozen at a time.

I can say "twelve" in Spanish pretty well, but "twenty-four" is out.

I might have trouble at Nancy's, I thought.

When I told Schumway about my predicament, he simply said, "Looks like you're going to have to make two trips."

"That's an idea," I said.

I do not mean to imply my friends at Nancy s cannot speak English—they can. But not as much as they speak Spanish, which seems only proper, considering the romance of the place.

In preparation for my trip to the tortilleria, I asked Gina Vasquez Cabral, a colleague of mine and linguist, to teach me how to say "twenty-four" in Spanish.

Having mastered that bit of skill, I set out for Nancy's.

When I arrived, Anastacio Garcia was there making flour tortillas. He and Lamberto Noriega, who is the head guy in the corn version of those circles of delight, begin their work each day at two in the morning.

They continue baking for 10 consecutive hours.

Among the women who help out is Manuela Almasan, who would brighten anyone's day

I placed my order with Nancy's father, ripping off "twenty-four" considerably well.

But I stumbled when I tried to tell him I wanted them in a paper bag instead of plastic.

Customers who came and went while I was there were Ramon Hernandez, who drops by every morning, and Maria Figueroa, a faithful customer for 11 years.

Having purchased my two dozen tortillas, I ventured over to Petra and Willie Lopez's El Merendero Bakery on Third Street for some bolillos and rosca.

Now I *really* have a language problem there. I point more than I speak when I visit El Merendero. Virtually no English is spoken there.

Eder Fernandez, who waits on me, is a kind and tolerant man.

"Twenty-four," of course, wouldn't work with Eder, because what would I do with two dozen loaves of bolillos?

So I just pointed and held up an index finger.

I completed the purchase, and as I walked out the door I encountered a nice man who said something to me in Spanish.

Obviously it was a friendly greeting.

I saw an immediate opportunity to apply my newly expanded vocabulary.

"*Veinticuatro,*" I responded in fluent Spanish—"twenty-four."

What the guy said about me to Eder after I left is not recorded.

Boris

If Boris Cherbak's and my service were converted to man-years, the record would show that he and I have been associated with the *Daily Bulletin* or its predecessors for nearly 80 years.

Some of our young colleagues have accused us of starting out with quill and bottled ink as well as type that was carved from wood.

That is not quite the whole truth, but an entire building full of gadgets, bells and blinks are part of our world now. They weren't around when Boris and I started out.

When he and I began, things were not as complicated—or simple—as they are now, depending on how one defines "technical advances."

To describe Boris as mechanically inclined or talented would be the worst sort of understatement. His mastery over things that whir, click, grind, pulsate, blink, hum or chug is carried out with unbelievable skill.

His natural ability is remarkable.

For years he has nursed newspaper presses through troubled times as a mother would see to the needs of a fevered child.

Boris has gentle hands that carry out functions originating in a mind of great order and plain sense. He is one of those guys who just *knows* what's wrong with something, and has the knack for making it right again.

He leans a lot less on books than he does on his own dependable and God-given instincts.

In the wintertime Boris wears a watch cap, making him look like a sailor on a ship arriving from Murmansk.

I've never seen Boris frown. His perpetual smile is as broad as the one worn by Alfred E. Newman, and his eyes join in the fun as they almost close entirely when he's really tickled.

Although we have known one another for years, I did not realize until recently that Boris and his family are attached to such an entrancing history.

The Cherbak bloodline and adventure flows to Russian nobility, political repression, escape to America, and local pioneering.

The Cherbaks are about as Russian as tea from a samovar, and if Boris' grandfather hadn't made the attempt to simplify things, Boris' last name would still be Stcherbakoff.

In the wintertime Boris wears a watch cap, making him look like a sailor on a ship arriving from Murmansk.

Boris' grandparents, Anton Peter and Sophia Cherbak, arrived in New York in 1898 with their seven children. Among the children was Boris' father, Boris Sr. An eighth child, George, was born later in what is now Alta Loma.

Anton had been a landowner in Russia, and had been an overseer of one of the Czar's estates. When the Czar refused to let Anton educate peasant families, Anton packed up his family and moved to America in search of greater freedom.

The family settled in Ioamosa, which Alta Loma was called at the time, and immediately began ranching.

Some of the Cherbaks' early-day dwellings still remain, including a large house built of river rock hauled from the canyons of the San Gabriels Mountains.

The original Cherbak stone house still stands today at 9983 Hillside Road in Rancho Cucamonga. The home was constructed nearly 86 years ago, and was designated a historical landmark in 1984.

None of the seven children or their parents who arrived in 1898 survive. But George, my friend Boris' uncle, is still living near Sacramento after spending most of his life in Alta Loma.

Some years after the family's arrival in America, Anton became a publisher of Russian language newspapers in Los Angeles and San Francisco. Following the Communist revolution, Anton felt his countrymen needed him, so he left his family in Alta Loma and returned to Russia where he tangled with the Reds.

He did not return.

"The family never did learn what happened to him," Boris told me, as his smile deserted him for a moment.

In his wake, however, Anton left a legacy of a ranch, a home and fine people.

Like my friend Boris.

The Monroe Street Parade

The love in Helen Tollefson's home sort of hangs there making its own song.

The good feeling seems to be suspended between her, her neighbors and her friends.

It is a love and admiration that runs deep, but is carried along on light hearts, smiles and a bounty of upbeat talk.

Her callers come by so frequently, an acquaintance of Helen told me, the place needs a revolving door. "It is a perpetual open house," said her old friend, Dorothy Rome. "Helen's a free spirit."

There is so much joy in the little house, one might believe there is hardly room for anything else. And that's just about right.

It's Helen's goodness that creates the scene.

"I like working with terminally ill patients —I think I'm good at helping them know when it's OK to go."

Describing her work and life would be like trying to deliver a speech about what makes a desert sunset so pretty. There's just a whole lot to it.

Last week Helen was honored at her small Pomona home by friends who helped her celebrate the 50th anniversary of the day she was capped—became a registered nurse.

The weekend party lasted all day and into the evening hours. She is 71 now, and as active as ever, serving full time with the West End Visiting Nurse Association, Support Services.

She has raised four children, and has worked nights most of her professional life ("I was always there when the kids came home").

Helen enthusiastically shared part of her life with me as she looked back on earlier times when she was paid $5 a day and when nurses "nursed" and cared for patients in a personal way.

"Those were the days before we started just pushing pills," she said, but added that she thinks nursing has completed a circle and there are many nurses now who are devoted to the "caring" aspect of their profession.

In her early career she worked with patients who were victims of infectious diseases—largely polio and tuberculosis.

She performed this service for many years at the Los Angeles County Hospital and the Veterans Hospital in San Fernando Valley.

Pomona became her home 11 years ago, not long after her husband died.

She told me she was drawn to patients with infectious diseases because she felt they were so isolated, set apart from and sometimes rejected by the public. She felt she was filling a void.

Helen herself lost some friendships when people became fearful of associating with her because of her exposure to contagious diseases.

Her empathy for ostracized patients has led her to regular volunteer work with AIDS patients in Los Angeles and the Inland Valley. She performs this impassioned work in addition to her regular job.

When I asked why she has stuck with nursing for more than 50 years, and intends to keep going, Helen smiled and said, "I like it. I really do.

"I like working with terminally ill patients—I think I'm good at helping them know when it's OK to go."

There's more to medicine than medicine, she said. "We need to help patients in body, mind and spirit. We must embrace a patient as a person. That's always been important to me."

This is selfless stuff, I thought.

Helen also teaches deep muscle massage techniques at the Cal Poly. "I don't deserve to have the knowledge if I don't share it."

A one-block-long parade was planned by friends on the day of Helen's party. I was invited to watch it go by.

Juan Gamboa, who cares for Helen's car at the neighborhood gas station, was going to decorate the vehicle and drive Helen down Monroe Street in front of her house.

The Monroe Street Parade.

"The parade was rained out," said friend Ruth Bobo of Claremont. "But we'll do it on the first really warm day."

I hope that day is soon. It's only right that the sun shines on Helen Tollefson's parade.

Leaving The Rest To Others

Thirty-nine years ago the world was pretty well at rest—at least measured against today's ripping events.

By 1955, World War II had begun to become real history.

The Korean War was freshly over, and our country was in a state of whew!

Dwight Eisenhower, who projected the image of a national father or grandfather, was president, and there was nothing much tearing away at our society.

Everybody liked Ike, even Democrats. Even Harry Truman.

There were more songs in more hearts than there are now.

Elvis was about to put music on a tilt, and Ed Sullivan was helping along the way.

I will miss those who have made my time here so—well—special. And I am grateful.

John Lennon was a 15-year-old kid in Liverpool where fame was waiting to track him down.

Bill Clinton was 8.

Southern California surfers rode swells to increasing popularity. "Wipeout" was about to become a real word.

All the sentinels along Euclid Avenue in Ontario were still the pepper trees that were planted there in 1883.

Mr. Roberts was playing at the Fox Theatre in Pomona, and a young performer named Jack Lemmon won an Oscar for best supporting actor in that movie.

Pomona and Ontario had only one high school each. They were Pomona High School on Holt Avenue (it burned down a few years later), and Chaffey High in Ontario, which is still there but tightly crowded.

Basque sheepherders still played handball behind the Centro Basco Hotel in Chino, Diamond Bar was still a ranch, and the Mexican players still whirled at Padua.

Fontana throbbed along with the Kaiser Steel plant where nearly 10,000 people labored in spark and fire.

The plant is mostly dust, dinge and broken brick now.

Most of what lay north of Foothill Boulevard through our valley was an great expanse of groves, but those trees were beginning their sad retreat before a relentless calendar.

A comparatively new freeway sliced through the valley in 1955. The superhighway was simply the Ramona Freeway in those days. It hurried east but petered out before it reached Redlands.

Gangs were largely limited to car clubs, and had not become the killing machines they are now.

Drugs were used by only the terribly troubled, and had not crawled onto high school and junior high school campuses to do their deadly work against a larger population.

Crime wasn't much, and cops still had time to help little kids across the street.

It was then that I began to chronicle the life and times of our community. Among the first events I was assigned to record involved three youngsters who were brand new Eagle Scouts.

It was a Page 1 story with picture in *The Daily Report*. It was that kind of time.

In the 39 years since then, I have written of a zillion events and people in our valley.

I have set down accounts of unfolding history with gritted teeth, sometimes with a smile, and once in a while with downright laughter.

I have written with tears, too.

But boredom has never been part of my work.

I have learned many things in those years. But none quite so well as the unbending truth that there is good in just about everyone.

Sometimes a lot of good.

Now it's time for me to leave what news people call the city room.

I am about to chase the adventure of retirement, leaving the grit, laughter and tears to others.

I will soon be leaving this pulsating place.

But they tell me being a writer is kind of like being left-handed—there's something permanent about it.

But for now I will miss the day to day chug of it all.

I will miss those who have made my time here so—well—special.

And I am grateful.

Epilogue

A few of the columns in this book require, I believe, some added information.

For example, a tragic event became part of the story about the young tagger whom I called Dako. Several weeks after the column was published, Dako was shot. He left the valley quietly, and returned, wounded, to his native Mexico. I never heard from him after our original talk, and I never knew who his assailant was.

The column about the death of the Kaiser Steel Mill in Fontana contained no specific information, of course, about what might happen to the plant's site. But now we know a state-of-the-art super motor speedway is being constructed there, and the track is scheduled to begin hosting big-league racing in 1997.

I wrote of former County Supervisor Dan Mikesell having a freeway interchange named for him, and I lamented the fact that no roadside sign was ever posted indicating the interchange had a name at all. Several months after the column was published, the state approved the placement of such a sign, and many dignitaries and friends gathered at the site to unveil it and to honor the former supervisor.

Regarding the column about my hospital stay, I finally learned that the mysterious nun who visited my room late each evening was indeed real and not an apparition. She was Sister Celine Mary Walsh, of St. Joseph's Catholic Church in Upland. I never saw her following her visits to me, but I learned months later who she was and that she had died. She was 85.

The column about the early history and high times of the Whispering Lakes Golf Course was written when the golf course was experiencing economic difficulty, and the course was in a state of general decay. The facility is now owned and operated by the City of Ontario, and it has been improved considerably in recent years. It boasts a much-improved course, restaurant, bar, banquet rooms and a well-stocked pro shop.

The piece about the problems of race relations in the valley and elsewhere made reference to Jay Kim, the then mayor of Diamond Bar. Since that column was written, Kim has been elected to the U.S. House of Representatives. He is the first Korean-born member of Congress.

The column about Dorothy Grant, the remarkable volunteer worker in Fontana, ended with Dorothy stating her wish that she had a little truck she could use in her volunteer work. Touched by the wish and by the work of Dorothy herself, County Supervisor Jon Mikels led an effort to make her wish come true. Several months after the original column was published, Mikels, at a surprise presentation, gave Dorothy the keys to a new truck as part of a federal block grant. Dorothy fainted.